# SANCTIFICATION;

OR,

# THE HIGHWAY OF HOLINESS.

AN ABRIDGMENT

*(IN THE AUTHOR'S OWN WORDS)*

OF

## THE GOSPEL MYSTERY OF SANCTIFICATION.

BY THE

## REV. WALTER MARSHALL.

LONDON:

JAMES NISBET & CO., 21 BERNERS STREET.

MDCCCLXXXIV.

# CONTENTS.

———◆◆———

|  |  | PAGE |
|---|---|---|
| INTRODUCTION | . . . . . . . . | V |
| CHAP. | | |
| I. OF THE KNOWLEDGE OF THE TRUE WAY OF HOLINESS | . | I |
| II. THE QUALIFICATIONS NEEDED FOR A HOLY LIFE | . . | 6 |
| III. HOLINESS IN CHRIST, AND UNION WITH HIM | . . | 10 |
| IV. FAITH AS THE MEANS OF UNION WITH CHRIST | . . | 21 |
| V. NO HOLINESS POSSIBLE IN THE NATURAL STATE | . . | 29 |
| VI. NO HOLINESS NEEDED TO GIVE A TITLE TO CHRIST | . | 32 |
| VII. NO HOLINESS NEEDED AS A PREPARATION FOR BELIEVING IN CHRIST | . . . . . . . . | 34 |
| VIII. NO HOLINESS BUT IN UNION WITH CHRIST | . . . | 37 |
| IX. NO HOLINESS WITHOUT FIRST ACCEPTING THE COMFORTS OF THE GOSPEL | . . . . . . . | 40 |
| X. NO HOLINESS WITHOUT SOME MEASURE OF ASSURANCE | | 42 |
| XI. THE DUTY OF BELIEVING AT ONCE AND BELIEVING ALWAYS | . . . . . . . . | 44 |
| XII. HOLINESS THROUGH FAITH | . . . . . | 52 |
| XIII. THE MEANS OF HOLINESS TO BE USED ONLY IN FAITH | | 69 |
| XIV. THE EXCELLENCE OF THIS WAY OF HOLINESS | . . | 77 |

THE

# HIGHWAY OF HOLINESS.

———◆———

## CHAPTER I.

### *OF THE KNOWLEDGE OF THE TRUE WAY OF HOLINESS.*

———

#### DIRECTION.

That we may acceptably perform the Duties of Holiness and
Righteousness required in the Law, our first Work is, to
learn *the Powerful and Effectual Means* whereby we may
attain to so great an End.

THIS Direction may serve, instead of a preface, to prepare
the understanding and attention of the reader for those
that follow. And,
*First*, It acquainteth you with *the great end* for which
all those means, that are the principal subject to be here
treated of, are designed. The scope of all is, to teach you
how you may attain to that practice and manner of life
which we call holiness, righteousness, or godliness, obedience, true religion ; and which God requireth of us in the
law, particularly in the moral law, which is summed up
in the ten commandments, and more briefly in those two
great commandments, of love to God and our neighbour

A

(Matt. xxii. 37, 39), and more largely explained throughout the Holy Scriptures. My work is, to show how the
duties of this law may be done when they are known;
therefore expect not that I should delay my intent, to
help you to the knowledge of them, by any large exposi-
tion of them. Yet that you may not miss the mark for
want of discerning it, take notice in few words, that the
holiness which I would bring you to, is *spiritual* (Rom.
vii. 14). It consists not only in external works of piety
and charity, but in the holy thoughts, imaginations, and
affections of the soul, and chiefly in love, from whence all
other good works must flow, or else they are not acceptable to God: not only in refraining the execution of sinful lusts, but in longing and delighting to do the will of
God, and in a cheerful obedience to God, without repin-
ing, fretting, grudging at any duty, as if it were a grievous
yoke and burden to you.

Take notice, further, that the law, which is your mark,
is *exceeding broad* (Ps. cxix. 96), and yet not the more
easy to be hit; because you must aim to hit it, in every
duty of it, with a performance of equal breadth, or else
you cannot hit it at all (Jas. ii. 10). The Lord is not at
all loved with that love that is due to Him as Lord of
all, if He be not loved with all our heart, spirit, and
might. We must love Him so as to yield ourselves
wholly up to His constant service in all things, and to
His disposal of us as our absolute Lord, whether it be for
prosperity or adversity, life or death.

This spiritual universal obedience is the great end to
the attainment whereof I am directing you. And that
you may not reject mine enterprise as impossible, observe,
that the most I promise is no more than *an acceptable
performance of these duties* of the law, such as our gracious
merciful God will certainly delight in, and be pleased
with, during our state of imperfection in this world, and
such as will end in perfection of holiness, and all happiness, in the world to come.

This is the true morality which God approveth of,

consisting in a conformity of all our actions to the
moral law. And if those that in these days contend so
highly for morality, do understand no other than this, I
dare join with them in asserting that the best morally
honest man is the greatest saint; and that morality is
the principal part of true religion, and the test of all
other parts, without which faith is dead, and all other
religious performances are a vain show and mere
hypocrisy.

The *second* thing contained in this introductory direction is, the necessity of learning the *powerful and
effectual means* whereby this great and excellent end
may be accomplished.

This is an advertisement very needful; because many
are apt to skip over the lesson concerning the *means*
(that will fill up this whole treatise) as superfluous and
useless. When once they know the nature and excellency of the duties of the law, they account nothing
wanting but diligent performances; and they rush blindly
upon immediate practice, making more haste than good
speed. They are quick in promising; "All that the
Lord hath spoken, we will do" (Exod. xix. 8), without
sitting down and counting the cost. They look upon
holiness as only the *means* to an end, eternal salvation;
not as *the end* itself, requiring any great means for
attaining the practice of it. The inquiry of most, when
they begin to have a sense of religion, is, "What good
thing shall I do that I may have eternal life?" (Matt.
xix. 16). Not, how shall I be enabled to do anything that is good? Yea many that are accounted powerful preachers, spend all their zeal in the earnest pressing
the immediate practice of the law, without any discovery
of the effectual means of performance; as if the works of
righteousness were like those servile employments that
need no skill and artifice at all, but only industry and
activity. That you may not stumble at the threshold of
a religious life by this common oversight, I shall
endeavour to make you sensible that it is not enough

for you to know the matter and reason of your duty, but that you are also to learn the powerful and effectual means of performance, before you can successfully apply yourselves to immediate practice.

Sanctification, whereby our hearts and lives are conformed to the law, is, equally with justification, a grace of God, communicated to us by means, and by means of teaching, and thereby learning something that we cannot see without the Word (Acts xxvi. 17, 18). There are several things pertaining to life and godliness that are given through knowledge (2 Pet. 1–3). There is a form of doctrine made use by God, to make people free from sin, and servants of righteousness (Rom. vi. 17, 18). Shall we slight and overlook the way of sanctification, when the learning the way of justification hath been accounted worth so many elaborate treatises?

The learning of it requireth double work; because we must unlearn many of our deeply-rooted notions, and become fools that we may be wise. We must pray earnestly to the Lord to teach us, as well as search the Scriptures that we may get this knowledge. " O that my ways were directed to keep Thy statutes! Teach me, O Lord, the way of Thy statutes, and I shall keep it unto the end " (Ps. cxix. 5, 33).

The certain knowledge of these powerful and effectual means is of great importance and necessity for our establishment in holy practice : for we cannot apply ourselves to the practice of holiness with hope of success, except we have some faith concerning the Divine assistance; which we have no ground to expect, if we use not such means as God hath appointed to work by. Many Christians content themselves with *external* performances, because they never knew how they might attain to *spiritual* service ; and many reject the way of holiness as austere and unpleasant, because they know not how to cut off a right hand, or pluck out a right eye, without intolerable pain ; whereas they would find " the ways of wisdom " (if they knew them) " to be ways of pleasantness, and all her paths to be peace" (Prov. iii. 17). Many others set upon the practice of holiness with a fervent zeal, and run very fast, but tread not a step in the right way ; and, finding themselves frequently disappointed and overcome by their lusts, they at last give over the work. Peradventure God may bless my discovery of the powerful means of holiness so far, as to save some one or other from killing themselves. And such a fruit as this would countervail my labour ; though I hope God will enlarge the hearts of many by it, to run with great cheerfulness, joy, and thanksgiving in the ways of His commandments.

# CHAPTER II.

## *THE QUALIFICATIONS NEEDED FOR A HOLY LIFE.*

### DIRECTION.

Several *Endowments and Qualifications* are necessary to enable
us for the immediate practice of the Law—particularly,

We must have *an inclination* and propensity of our hearts
thereunto ;

And therefore we must be well *persuaded of our Reconciliation
with God,*

And of *our future enjoyment* of the Everlasting Happiness,

And of *sufficient strength* both to will and perform all duties
acceptably, until we come to the Enjoyment of that Happiness.

I HAVE named here several qualifications and endowments
that are necessary to make up *that holy frame and state
of the soul,* whereby it is furnished and enabled to practise the law immediately, and that not only in the beginning, but in the continuation of that practice. The first
Adam had excellent endowments bestowed upon him for
an holy practice, when he was first created according to
the image of God ; and the second Adam had endowments more excellent, to enable Him for an harder task
of obedience. And seeing obedience is grown more difficult, by reason of the opposition and temptations that it
meeteth with since the fall of Adam, we that are to be
imitators of Christ had need have very choice endowments,

as Christ had ; at least as good or something better than Adam had at first, as our work is harder than his.

That none may deceive themselves, and miscarry in their enterprise for holiness, by depending on such a weak occult quality, I have here showed FOUR ENDOW-MENTS, of which *a true ability for the practice of holiness* must necessarily be constituted, and by which it must subsist and be maintained, intending to show afterwards by what means these endowments are given to us, and whether the inclination or propensity here mentioned be perfect or imperfect.

In the *first* place, I assert that *an inclination and propensity of heart* to the duties of the law is necessary to frame and enable us for the immediate practice of them.

The duties of the law are of such a nature that they cannot possibly be performed while there is wholly an aversion or mere indifference of the heart to the performance of them, and no good inclination and propensity towards the practice of them ; because the chief of all the commandments is to love the Lord with our whole heart, might, and soul, to love everything that is in Him, to love His will, and all His ways, and to like them as good. And all duties must be influenced in their performance by this love. We must delight to do the will of God ; it must be sweeter to us than the honey or honey-comb (Ps. xl. 8 ; Job xxiii. 12 ; Ps. lxiii. 1, cxix. 20, and xix. 10). And this love, liking, delight, longing, thirsting, sweet-relishing, must be continued to the end; and the first indeliberate motion of lust must be regulated by love to God and our neighbour ; and sin must be lusted against (Gal. v. 17), and abhorred (Ps. xxxvi. 4). Love to God must flow from a clean heart (1 Tim. i. 5), a heart cleansed from evil· propensities and inclinations. And reason will tell us that the first motions of lust, which fall not under our choice and deliberation, cannot be avoided without a fixed propensity of the heart to holiness.

The *second* ENDOWMENT necessary to enable us for the immediate practice of holiness is, that we be *well persuaded of our reconciliation with God.*

God hath abundantly discovered to us in His Word that His method in bringing men from sin to holiness of life is first to make them know that He loveth them, and that their sins are blotted out.

The *third* ENDOWMENT necessary to enable us for the practice of holiness, without which a persuasion of our reconciliation with God would be of little efficacy to work in us a rational propensity to it, is, that *we be persuaded of our future enjoyment of the everlasting heavenly happiness.* This must precede our holy practice, as a cause disposing and alluring us to it.

Christ, the great pattern of holiness, "for the joy that was set before Him, endured the cross, despising the shame" (Heb. xii. 2). The apostles did not faint under affliction, because they knew that it wrought for them "a far more exceeding and eternal weight of glory" (2 Cor. iv. 16, 17). As worldly hope keepeth the world at work in their various employments, so God giveth His people the hope of His glory, to keep them close to His service (Heb. vi. 11, 12; 1 John iii. 3). The way for us to keep ourselves in the love of God is to look for His mercy unto eternal life (Jude, verse 21).

The *last* ENDOWMENT, for the same end as the former, is, that we be *well persuaded of sufficient strength both to will and perform* our duty acceptably, until we come to the enjoyment of the heavenly happiness.

Those that think sincere conformity to the law in ordinary cases to be so very easy, show that they neither know it nor themselves. I acknowledge that the work of God is easy and pleasant to those whom God rightly furnisheth with endowments for it; but those that assert it to be easy to men in their common condition, show their imprudence in contradicting the general experience of heathens and Christians.

The wisdom of God hath ever furnished people with a good persuasion of a *sufficient strength* that they might be enabled both to will and to do their duty. The first Adam was furnished with such a strength. Our Lord Christ doubtless knew the infinite power of His deity to enable Him for all that He was to do and suffer in our nature. He knew " the Lord God would help Him, and that therefore He should not be confounded" (Isa. l. 7). The Scripture showeth what plentiful assurance of strength God gave to Moses, Joshua, Gideon, when He called them to great employments ; and to the Israelites when He called them to subdue the land of Canaan. Paul encourageth believers to the life of holiness by per-suading them that sin shall not prevail to get the dominion over them, because "they are not under the law, but under grace" (Rom. vi. 13, 14). And he exhorteth them "to be strong in the Lord, and in the power of His might, that they might be able to stand against the wiles of the devil" (Eph. vi. 10, 11). John exhorteth believers "not to love the world, nor the things of the world, because they were strong, and had overcome the wicked one" (1 John ii. 14, 15). They that were called of God heretofore to work miracles were first acquainted with the gift of power to work them ; and no wise man will attempt to do them without knowledge of the gift ; even so, when men that are dead in sin are called to do the works of a holy life, which are in them great miracles, God maketh a discovery of *the gift of power* unto them, that He may encourage them in a rational way to such a wonderful enterprise.

# CHAPTER III.

## *HOLINESS IN CHRIST AND UNION WITH HIM.*

———

### DIRECTION.

The way to get Holy Endowments and Qualifications necessary to frame and enable us for the immediate practice of the Law is, *to receive them out of the fulness of Christ by fellowship with Him;*

And that we may have this fellowship, we must *be in Christ, and have Christ Himself in us,* by a mystical union with Him.

HERE, as much as anywhere, we have great cause to acknowledge with the apostle, that, "without controversy great is the mystery of godliness," even so great that it could "not have entered into the heart of man to conceive it, if God had not made it known" in the gospel by supernatural revelation. Yea, though it be revealed clearly in the Holy Scriptures, yet the natural man has not eyes to see it there, for it is foolishness to him; and if God express it ever so plainly and properly, he will think that God is speaking riddles and parables. And I doubt not but it is still a riddle and parable even to many truly godly, who have received an holy nature in this way; for the apostles themselves had the saving benefit of it before the Comforter discovered it clearly to them (John xiv. 20).

One great mystery is, that *the holy frame and disposi-*

*tion,* whereby our souls are furnished and enabled for immediate practice of the law, must be obtained "by receiving it out of Christ's fulness," *as a thing already prepared and brought to an existence for us in Christ,* and treasured up in Him ; and that, as we are justified by a righteousness wrought out in Christ, and imputed to us, so we are sanctified by such *an holy frame* and qualifications as are first *wrought out and completed in Christ for us,* and then *imparted to us.* And as our natural corruption was produced originally in the first Adam, and propagated from him to us, so our new nature and holiness is first produced in Christ, and derived from Him to us, or, as it were, propagated. So that we are not at all to work together with Christ in making or producing that holy frame in us, but *only to take it* to ourselves, and use it in our holy practice, as made ready to our hands. Thus we have fellowship with Christ in receiving that holy frame of spirit that was originally in Him ; for fellowship is when several persons have the same things in common (1 John i. 1-3).

This mystery is so great that, notwithstanding all the light of the gospel, we commonly think that we must get an holy frame by producing it anew in ourselves, and by forming it and working it out of our own hearts. Therefore many that are seriously devout take a great deal of pains to mortify their corrupted nature, and beget an holy frame of heart in themselves by striving earnestly to master their sinful lusts, and by pressing vehemently upon their hearts many motives to godliness, labouring importunately to squeeze good qualifications out of them, as oil out of a flint. They account that though they be justified by a righteousness wrought out by Christ, yet they must be sanctified by a holiness wrought out by themselves. And though out of humility they are willing to call it infused grace, yet they think they must get the infusion of it by the same manner of working, as if it were wholly acquired by their endeavours. On this account they acknowledge the entrance into a godly life to be harsh and unpleasing, because it costs so much struggling with their own hearts and affections to new-frame them.    If they knew that this way of entrance is not only harsh and unpleasant, but altogether impossible ; and that the true way of mortifying sin and quickening themselves to holiness is by receiving a new nature out of the fulness of Christ ; and that we do no more to the production of a new nature than of original sin, though we do more to the reception of it.    If they knew this they might save themselves many a bitter agony, and a great deal of misspent burdensome labour, and employ their endeavours to enter in at the strait gate in such a way as would be more pleasant and successful.

Another great mystery in the way of sanctification is the *glorious manner of our fellowship* with Christ, in receiving an holy frame of heart from Him.    It is by being in Christ, and having Christ Himself in us,—and that not merely by His universal presence as He is God, but by such a close union as that we are one spirit and one flesh with Him,—which is a privilege peculiar to those that are truly sanctified.    I may well call this a mystical union, because the apostle calleth it a great mystery, in an epistle full of mysteries (Eph. v. 32), intimating that it is eminently great above many other mysteries.    This union betwixt Christ and believers is plain from several places of Scripture, which testify that Christ is and dwelleth in believers, and they in Him (John vi. 56, and xiv. 20), and that they are so joined together as to become one spirit (1 Cor. vi. 17), and that believers are members of Christ's body, of His flesh, and of His bones; and that they two, Christ and the Church, are one flesh (Eph. v. 30, 31).    Furthermore, this union is illustrated in Scripture by various resemblances which would be very much unlike the things which they are made use of to resemble, and would rather seem to beguile us by obscuring the truth, than instruct us by illustrating of it, if there were no true, proper union, between Christ and

believers. It is resembled by the union between God
the Father and Christ (John xiv. 20, and xvii. 21–23),
between the vine and its branches (John xv. 4, 5), between the head and the body (Eph. i. 22, 23), between
bread and the eater (John vi. 51–54). It is not only
resembled, but sealed in the Lord's Supper—where
neither the Popish transubstantiation, nor the Lutheran's
consubstantiation, nor the Protestant's spiritual presence
of Christ's body and blood to the true receivers, can stand
without it. And, if we can imagine that Christ's body
and blood are not truly eaten and drunk by believers,
either spiritually or corporeally, we shall make the bread
and wine joined with the words of institution not only
naked signs, but such signs as are much more apt to breed
false notions in us than to establish us in the truth. And
there is nothing in this union so impossible or repugnant
to reason, as may force us to depart from the plain and
familiar sense of those Scriptures that express and illustrate it. Though Christ be in heaven and we on earth,
yet He can join our souls and bodies to His at such a
distance, without any substantial change of either, by the
same infinite Spirit dwelling in Him and us; and so our
flesh will become His when it is quickened by His Spirit,
and His flesh ours, as truly as if we did eat His flesh and
drink His blood; and He will be in us Himself by His
Spirit, who is one with Him, and who can make a more
close and intimate union between Christ and us than any
material substance can do.

And it will not follow from hence that a believer is one
person with Christ. Neither will a believer be necessarily
perfect in holiness hereby, or Christ made a sinner: for
Christ knoweth how to dwell in believers by certain
measures and degrees, and to make them holy so far only
as He dwelleth in them.

Having thus far explained the direction, I shall now
show that though the truth contained in it be above the
reach of natural reason, yet it is evidently discovered to
those that have their understandings opened to discern

that supernatural revelation of the mysterious way of sanctification which God hath given to us in the Holy Scriptures.

1. There are several places in Scripture that do plainly express it. Some texts show that all things pertaining to our salvation are treasured up for us in Christ, and comprehended in His fulness; so that we must have them thence or not at all (Col. i. 19). "It pleased the Father that in Him should all fulness dwell." And, in the same epistle (Col. ii. 11-13), the apostle showeth that the holy nature whereby we live to God was first produced in us by His death and resurrection: "In whom also ye are circumcised in putting off the body of the sins of the flesh; buried with him; quickened together with Him; when ye were dead in your sins." And again in Eph. i. 3, he testifies that "God hath blessed us with all spiritual blessings in heavenly places in Christ." An holy frame of spirit, with all its necessary qualifications, must needs be comprehended here in "all spiritual blessings;" and these are given us in Christ's person in heavenly places, as prepared and treasured up in Him for us while we are upon earth; and therefore we must have our holy endowments out of Him or not at all.

Other texts of Scripture show plainly that we receive our holiness out of His fulness by fellowship with Him, (John i. 16, 17): "Of His fulness have all we received, and grace for grace"—in which Scripture the grace spoken of as received from Christ, being answerable to "the law given by Moses" in the preceding clause, must needs include the grace of sanctification. Again we read (1 John i. 3, 5-7): "Truly our fellowship is with the Father, and with His Son Jesus Christ. God is light. If we walk in the light, as He is in the light, we have fellowship one with another." Whence we may infer that our fellowship with God and Christ doth include particularly our having light, and walking in it holily and righteously. There are other texts that reach the proof of the whole direction fully; showing, not only that our holy endowments are made ready first in Christ for us, and received from Christ, but that we receive them by union with Christ: Col. iii. 10, 11, "Ye have put on the new man, which is renewed after the image of Him that created him; where Christ is all and in all;" 1 Cor. vi. 17, "He that is joined to the Lord is one spirit;" Gal. ii. 20, "I live; yet not I, but Christ liveth in me;" 1 John v. 11, 12, "This is the record, that God hath given to us eternal life; and this life is in His Son. He that hath the Son hath life, and he that hath not the Son hath not life." Can we desire that God should more clearly teach us that all the fulness of the new man, and all that spiritual nature and life whereby we live to God in holiness, is in Christ; and that they are fixed in Him so inseparably that we cannot have them except we be joined to Him, and have Himself abiding in us?

2. God is pleased to illustrate this mysterious manner of our sanctification by such variety of similitudes and resemblances as may put us out of doubt that it is truth, and such a truth as we are highly concerned to know and believe. I shall endeavour to contract the chief of these resemblances, and the force of them, briefly into one sentence, leaving it to those that are spiritual to enlarge their meditation upon them. We receive from Christ a new holy frame and nature, whereby we are enabled for an holy practice, by union and fellowship with Him; in like manner, 1. As Christ lived in our nature by the Father (John vi. 57); 2. As we receive original sin and death propagated to us from the first Adam (Rom. v. 12, 14, 16, 17); 3. As the natural body receiveth sense, motion, nourishment from the head (Col. ii. 19); 4. As the branch receiveth its sap, juice, and fructifying virtue from the vine (John xv. 4, 5); 5. As the wife bringeth forth fruit by virtue of her conjugal union with her husband (Rom. vii. 4); 6. As stones become an holy temple by being built upon the foundation and joined with the chief corner-stone (1 Pet. ii. 4, 5, 7); 7. As we receive the nourishing virtue of bread by eating

it, and of wine by drinking it (John vi. 51, 55, 57), which last resemblance is used to seal to us our communion with Christ in the Lord's Supper. Here are seven resemblances instanced, whereof some do illustrate the mystery spoken of more fully than others: all of them do some way intimate that *our new life and holy nature* is first in Christ, and then in us by a true, proper union and fellowship with Him. If any should urge that the similitudes of Adam and his seed, and of married couples, do make rather for a relative than a real union betwixt Christ and us, let them consider that all nations are really made of one blood, which was first in Adam (Acts xvii. 26), and that the first woman was made out of the body of Adam, and was really bone of his bone, and flesh of his flesh. And by this first married couple the mystical union of Christ and His Church is eminently resembled (Gen. ii. 22–24, with Eph. v. 30–32). And yet it surpasseth both these resemblances in the nearness and fulness of them; because those that are joined to the Lord are not only one flesh but one spirit with Him.

3. The end of Christ's incarnation, death, and resurrection was *to prepare and form an holy nature and frame for us in Himself, to be communicated to us by union and fellowship with Him, and not to enable us to produce in ourselves the first original of such an holy nature by our own endeavours.*

(1.) By His *incarnation* there was a man created in a new holy frame, after the holiness of the first Adam's frame had been marred and abolished by the first transgression; and this *new frame* was far more excellent than ever the first Adam's was, because man was really joined to God by a close inseparable union of the divine and human nature in one person—Christ; so that these natures had communion each with other in their actings, and Christ was able to act in His human nature by power proper to the divine nature, wherein He was one God with the Father. Why was it that Christ set up the

fallen *nature of man in such a wonderful frame of holi-*
*ness, in bringing it to live and act by communion with God*
*living and acting in it?* One great end was *that He*
*might communicate this excellent frame to His seed* that
should by His Spirit be born of Him and be in Him as
the last Adam, the quickening Spirit; that, as we have
borne the image of the earthly man so we might also bear
the image of the heavenly (1 Cor. xv. 45, 49), in holiness
here and in glory hereafter. Thus He was born Emma-
nuel, God with us; because *the fulness of the Godhead,*
*with all holiness, did first dwell* in Him bodily, even *in*
*His human nature,* that we might be filled with that fulness in Him (Matt. i. 23; Col. ii. 9, 10). Thus He came
down from heaven as living bread, that, as He liveth by
the Father, so those that eat Him may live by Him (John
vi. 51, 57); by *the same life of God in them* that was
first in Him.

(2.) By His *death* He freed Himself from the guilt of
our sins imputed to Him, and from all that innocent
weakness of His human nature which He had borne for
a time for our sakes. And, by freeing Himself, He *pre-*
*pared a freedom for us from our whole natural condition;*
which is both weak as His was, and also polluted with
our guilt and sinful corruption. Thus the corrupt natural
estate, which is called in Scripture the "old man," was
crucified together with Christ, that the body of sin might
be destroyed. And it is destroyed in us, not by any
wounds that we ourselves can give to it, but by our partaking of that freedom from it, and death unto it, that *is*
*already wrought out for us* by the death of Christ; as is
signified by our baptism, wherein we are buried with
Christ by the application of His death to us (Rom. vi.
2, 3, 4, 10, 11).

God "sending His own Son in the likeness of sinful
flesh, for sin" (or, "by a sacrifice for sin," as in the margin),
"condemned sin in the flesh: that the righteousness of the
law might be fulfilled in us, who walk not after the flesh,
but after the Spirit" (Rom. viii. 3, 4). Observe here,

B

that though Christ died that we might be justified by the righteousness of God and of faith, not by our own righteousness, which is of the law (Rom. x. 4–6; Phil. iii. 9), yet *He died also*, that the righteousness of the law might be fulfilled *in* us, and *that* by walking after His Spirit, as those that are in Christ (Rom. viii. 4). He is resembled in His death to a corn of wheat dying in the earth, that it may propagate its own nature by bringing forth much fruit (John xii. 24); to the passover that was slain, that a feast might be kept upon it; and to bread broken, that it may be nourishment to those that eat it (1 Cor. v. 7, 8, and xi. 24); to the rock smitten, that water might gush out of it for us to drink (1 Cor. x. 4).

He died that He might make, of Jew and Gentile, one new man in Himself (Eph. ii. 15); and that He might see His seed, *i.e.*, such as derive their holy nature from Him (Isa. liii. 10). Let these Scriptures be well observed, and they will sufficiently evidence that Christ died, not that we might be able to form an holy nature in ourselves, but that we might *receive one ready prepared and formed in Christ for us*, by union and fellowship with Him.

(3.) By His *resurrection*. He took possession of spiritual life for us, as now fully procured for us, and made to be our right and property by the merit of His death; and therefore we are said to be quickened together with Christ. His resurrection was our resurrection to the life of holiness, as Adam's fall was our fall into spiritual death. And we are not ourselves the first makers and formers of our new holy nature, any more than of our original corruption, but both are formed ready for us to partake of them. And, by union with Christ, we partake of that spiritual life that He took possession of for us at His resurrection, and thereby we are enabled to bring forth the fruits of it; as the Scripture showeth by the similitude of a marriage union. Rom. vii. 4, "We are married to Him that is raised from the dead, that we might bring forth fruit unto God."

4. Our sanctification is *by the Holy Ghost*, by whom

we live and walk holily (Rom. xv. 16; Gal. v. 25). Now the Holy Ghost first rested on Christ in all fulness, that He might be communicated from Him to us. And when He sanctifieth us, He baptizeth us into Christ, and joineth us to Christ by Himself, as the great bond of union (1 Cor. xii. 13). So that, according to the Scriptural phrase, it is all one to have Christ Himself, and to have the Spirit of Christ in us (Rom. viii. 9, 10). " He glorifieth Christ; for He receiveth those things that are Christ's, and showeth them to us" (John xvi. 14, 15). He giveth us an experimental knowledge of those spiritual blessings which He Himself prepared for us by the incarnation, death, and resurrection of Christ.

5. The effectual causes of those four principal endowments, which, in the foregoing direction, were asserted as necessary to furnish us for the immediate practice of holiness, are comprehended in the fulness of Christ, and treasured up for us in Him; and the endowments themselves, together with their causes, are attained richly by union and fellowship with Christ. If we be joined to Christ, our hearts will be no longer left under the power of sinful inclinations, or in a mere indifferency of inclination to good or evil; but they will be powerfully endued with a power, bent, and propensity to the practice of holiness, by the Spirit of Christ dwelling in us, and inclining us to mind spiritual things, and not to lust after the flesh (Rom. viii. 1, 4, 5; Gal. v. 17).

And we have in Christ a full reconciliation with God, and an advancement into higher favour with Him, than the first Adam had in the state of innocency; because the righteousness that Christ wrought out for us by His obedience unto death, is imputed to us for our justification. And, that we may be persuaded of this reconciliation, we receive the Spirit of adoption through Christ, whereby we cry, Abba, Father (Rom. viii. 15).

Hereby also we are persuaded of our future enjoyment of the everlasting happiness, and of sufficient strength both to will and to perform our duty acceptably, until we come to that enjoyment. For the Spirit of adoption teacheth us to conclude, that, if we be the children of God, then we are heirs of God, and joint heirs with Christ; and that the law of the spirit of life that is in Christ Jesus, maketh us free from the law of sin and death; and that nothing shall be against us, nothing shall separate us from the love of God in Christ, but, in opposition and difficulties that we meet with, we shall be at last more than conquerors through Him that loved us (Rom. viii. 2, 17, 35, 37, 39).

Furthermore, this comfortable persuasion of our justification and future happiness, and all saving privileges, cannot tend to licentiousness, as it is given only in this way of union with Christ; because it is joined inseparably with the gift of sanctification, by the Spirit of Christ; so that we cannot have justification, or any saving privilege in Christ, except we receive Christ Himself, and His holiness as well as any other benefit; as the Scripture testifieth, that " There is no condemnation to them which are in Christ Jesus, who walk not after the flesh, but after the Spirit" (Rom. viii. 1).

# CHAPTER IV.

*FAITH AS THE MEANS OF UNION WITH CHRIST.*

---

## DIRECTION.

*The Means or Instruments* whereby the Spirit of God accomplisheth our union with Christ, and our fellowship with Him in all holiness, are,

*The Gospel,* whereby Christ entereth into our hearts to work faith in us ;

And *faith,* whereby we actually receive Christ Himself, with all His fulness into our hearts.

And this faith is a grace of the Spirit, whereby we heartily *believe the Gospel,* and *also believe on Christ,* as He is revealed and freely promised to us therein, for all His salvation.

THAT which I asserted in the foregoing direction concerning the necessity of our being in Christ, and having Christ in us, by a mystical union, to enable us for an holy practice, might put us to a stand in our endeavours for holiness ; because we cannot imagine how we should be able to raise ourselves above our natural sphere to this glorious union and fellowship, until God be pleased to make known to us, by supernatural revelation, the means whereby His Spirit maketh us partakers of so high a privilege. But God is pleased to help us at a stand to go on forward, by revealing two means or instruments whereby His Spirit accomplisheth the mystical union and fellowship between Christ and us, and whereby rational creatures are capable of attaining thereunto by His Spirit working in them.

One of these means is "the gospel of the grace of God," wherein God doth make known unto us the unsearchable riches of Christ, and Christ in us, the hope of glory (Eph. iii. 8; Col. i. 27); and doth also invite us and command us to believe on Christ for His salvation, and doth encourage us by a free promise of that salvation to all that believe on Him (Acts xiii. 38, 39; Rom. x. 9, 11.) This is God's own *instrument of conveyance,* wherein He sendeth Christ to us to bless us with His salvation (Acts iii. 26). It is the ministration of the Spirit and of righteousness (2 Cor. iii. 6, 8, 9). Faith cometh by the hearing of it; and therefore it is a great instrument whereby we are begotten in Christ, and Christ is formed in us (Rom. x. 16, 17; 1 Cor. iv. 15; Gal. iv. 19).

The word is nigh to us, the gospel, the word of faith, in which Christ Himself graciously condescendeth to be nigh to us; so that we may come at Him there, without going any further, if we desire to be joined to Him (Rom. x. 6–8).

The other of the means is faith, that is wrought in us by the gospel. This is our *instrument of reception,* whereby the union between Christ and us is accomplished on our part, by our actual receiving Christ Himself, with all His fulness, into our hearts, which is the principal subject of the present explanation.

Saving faith must necessarily contain two acts—believing the truth of the gospel, and believing on Christ, as promised freely to us in the gospel for all salvation. By the one it receiveth the means, wherein Christ is conveyed to us—by the other, it receiveth Christ Himself and His salvation in the means; as it is one act to receive the breast or cup wherein milk or wine are conveyed, and another act to suck the milk in the breast and to drink the wine in the cup. And both these acts must be performed heartily, with an unfeigned love to the truth, and a desire of Christ and His salvation above all things. This is our spiritual appetite, which is necessary for our eating and drinking Christ, the food of life, as a natural appetite is for bodily nourishment. The former of these acts doth not immediately unite us to Christ, because it is terminated only on the means of conveyance, the gospel; yet it is a saving act, if it be rightly performed, because it inclineth and disposeth the soul to the latter act, whereby Christ Himself is immediately received into the heart. He that believeth the gospel with hearty love and liking as the most excellent truth, will certainly with the like heartiness believe on Christ for His salvation. "They that know the name of the Lord will certainly put their trust in Him" (Ps. ix. 10). Therefore, in Scripture, saving faith is sometimes described by the former of these acts, as if it were a mere believing the gospel; sometimes by the latter, as a believing on Christ or in Christ—Rom. x. 9, "If thou believe in thine heart that God raised Him from the dead, thou shalt be saved." Ver. 11, "The Scripture saith, that whosoever believeth on Him shall not be ashamed."

Having thus explained the nature of faith, I come now to assert its proper use and office in our salvation—that it is the means and instrument whereby we receive Christ, and all His fulness, actually into our hearts. This excellent use and office of faith is encountered by a multitude of errors. Some will allow that faith is the sole condition of our justification, and the instrument to receive it; but they account that it is not sufficient or effectual to sanctification, but that it rather tendeth to licentiousness, if it be not joined with some other means that may be powerful and effectual to secure an holy practice.

All these errors will fall, if it can be proved that such a faith as I have described is an instrument whereby we actually receive Christ Himself into our hearts, and holiness of heart and life, as well as justification, by union and fellowship with Him. For the proof of it I shall offer the following arguments:—

1. By faith we have the actual enjoyment and posses-

sion of Christ Himself, and not only of remission of sins, but of life, and so of holiness. " Christ dwelleth in our hearts by faith" (Eph. iii. 17). We live to God, and yet not we, but "Christ liveth in us by the faith of the Son of God" (Gal. ii. 19, 20). " He that believeth on the Son of God hath the Son, and everlasting life that is in Him" (1 John v. 12, 13; John iii. 36).

2. The Scripture plainly ascribeth this effect to faith, that by it we receive Christ, put Him on, are rooted and grounded in Him; and also, that we receive the Spirit, remission of sins, and an inheritance among all them which are sanctified (John i. 12; Gal. iii. 26, 27; Col. ii. 6, 7; Gal. iii. 14; Acts xxvi. 18). And the Scripture illustrateth this receiving by the similitude of eating and drinking; he that believeth on Christ, drinketh the living water, or His Spirit, as in John vii. 37-39; Christ is the bread of life; His flesh is meat indeed, and His blood is drink indeed. And the way to eat and drink it is to believe in Christ; and by so doing, we dwell in Christ, and Christ in us, and have everlasting life (John vi. 35, 47, 48, 54-56). How can it be taught more clearly, that we receive Christ Himself properly into our souls by faith, as we do receive food into our bodies by eating and drinking, and that Christ is as truly united to us thereby, as our food is when we eat or drink it?

3. Christ, with all His salvation, is freely given by the grace of God to all that believe on Him. For " we are saved by grace through faith; and that not of ourselves; it is the gift of God " (Eph. ii. 8, 9). The condition of a free gift is only, Take and have. The free offer of Christ to you is sufficient to confer upon you a right, yea, to make it your duty so receive Christ and His salvation as yours. And, because we receive Christ by faith as a free gift, therefore we may account faith to be the instrument, and, as it were, the hand whereby we receive Him.

4. It hath been already proved, that all spiritual life and holiness is treasured up in the fulness of Christ, and communicated to us by union with him. Therefore the

accomplishing of union with Christ is the first work of saving grace in our hearts. And faith itself being an holy grace, and part of spiritual life, cannot be in us before the beginning of that life; but rather it is given to us, and wrought in us in the very working of the union.

5. True saving faith, such as I have described, hath in its nature and manner of operation a peculiar aptitude or fitness to receive Christ and His salvation, and to unite our souls to Him; and to furnish the soul with a new holy nature, and to bring forth an holy practice by union and fellowship with Him. God hath fitted natural instruments for their office, as the hands, feet, &c., so that we may know, by their nature and natural manner of operation, for what use they are designed. In like manner we may know that faith is an instrument formed on purpose for our union with Christ, and for sanctification, if we consider what a peculiar fitness it hath for the work. The discovery of this is of great use for the understanding of the mysterious manner of our receiving and practising all holiness by union and fellowship with Christ, by this precious grace of faith.

There is in this saving faith a natural tendency to furnish the soul with an holy frame or nature, and all endowments necessary thereunto, out of the fulness of Christ. An hearty, affectionate trusting on Christ for all His salvation, as freely promised to us, hath naturally enough in it to work in our souls a rational bent and inclination to, and ability for, the practice of all holiness; because it comprehendeth in it a trusting, that, through Christ, we are dead to sin, and alive to God, and that our old man is crucified (Rom. vi. 2-4); and that we live by the Spirit (Gal. v. 25); and that we have forgiveness of sin; and that God is our God (Ps. xxxi. 14); and that we have in the Lord righteousness and strength, whereby we are able to do all things (Isa. xlv. 24; Phil. iv. 13).

Because faith hath such a natural tendency to dispose and strengthen the soul for the practice of holiness, we have cause to judge it a meet instrument to accomplish every part of that practice in an acceptable manner. Those that with a due affection believe steadfastly on Christ for the free gift of all His salvation, may find by experience that they are carried forth by that faith, according to the measure of its strength or weakness, to love God heartily, because God hath loved them first (1 John iv. 19); to praise Him, to pray unto Him in the name of Christ (Eph. v. 20; John xvi. 26, 27); to be patient with cheerfulness under all afflictions, giving thanks to the Father, that hath called them to His heavenly inheritance (Col. i. 11, 12); to love all the children of God, out of love to their heavenly Father (1 John v. 1); to walk as Christ walked (1 John ii. 6); and to give themselves up to live to Christ in all things, as constrained by His love in dying for them (2 Cor. v. 14). We have a cloud of witnesses concerning the excellent works that were produced by faith (Heb. xi.) Though trusting on Christ be accounted such a slight and contemptible thing, yet I know no work of obedience which it is not able to produce. And note the excellent *manner* of working by faith. By it we live and act in all good works, as people in Christ, as raised above ourselves and our natural state, by partaking of Him and His salvation ; and we do all in His name and on His account. This is the practice of that mysterious manner of living to God in holiness, which is peculiar to the Christian religion, wherein we live, and yet not we, but Christ liveth in us (Gal. ii. 20). And who can imagine any other way but this for such a practice, while Christ and His salvation is known to us only by the gospel?

I shall add something concerning the efficient cause of this excellent grace, and of our union with Christ by it, whereby it may appear that it is not so slight and easy a way of salvation as some may imagine. The author and finisher of our faith, and of our union and fellowship with Christ by faith, is no less than the infinite Spirit of God, and God and Christ Himself by the Spirit; "by one Spirit we are all baptized into one body of Christ, and are all made to drink into one Spirit" (1 Cor. xii. 12, 13). God granteth us, according to the riches of His glory, to be strengthened with all might by His Spirit in the inner man, that Christ may dwell in our hearts by faith (Eph. iii. 16, 17). If we do but consider the great effect of faith, that by it we are raised to live above our natural condition, by Christ and His Spirit living in us, we cannot rationally conceive that it should be within the power of nature to do anything that advanceth us so high. If God had done no more for us in our sanctification than to restore us to our first natural holiness, yet this could not have been done without putting forth His own almighty power to quicken those that are dead in sin; how much more is this almighty power needful to advance us to this wonderful new kind of frame, wherein we live and act above all the power of nature, by a higher principle of life than was given to Adam in innocency, even by Christ and His Spirit living and acting in us? So He taketh us into mystical union and fellowship with Himself by no less than an infinite creating power.

For the accomplishing this great work of our new creation in Christ, the Spirit of God doth first work upon our hearts by and with the gospel to produce in us the grace of faith. We shall never come to Christ by any teaching of man except we also hear and learn of the Father, and be drawn to Christ by His Spirit (John vi. 44, 45). And, when saving faith is wrought in us, the same Spirit giveth us a firm hold of Christ by it. As He openeth the mouth of faith to receive Christ, so He filleth it with Christ; or else the acting of faith would be like a dream of one that thinketh he eateth and drinketh, and when he awaketh he findeth himself empty. The same Spirit of God did both give that faith whereby miracles were wrought, and did work also the miracles by it; so also the same Spirit of Christ doth work saving faith in us, and doth answer the aim and end of that faith by giving us union and fellowship with Christ by it, so that none of the glory of this work belongeth to faith, but only to Christ and His

Spirit. And, indeed, faith is of such an humble, self-denying nature, that it ascribeth nothing that it receiveth to itself, but all to the grace of God ; and, therefore, God saveth us by faith that all the glory may be ascribed to His free grace (Rom. iv. 16).

Thus are we first passive and then active in this great work of mystical union; we are first apprehended of Christ, and then we apprehend Christ. Christ entereth first into the soul, to join Himself to it, by giving it the Spirit of faith ; and so the soul receiveth Christ and His Spirit by their own power—as the sun first enlighteneth our eyes, and then we can see it by its own light.

# CHAPTER V.

## *NO HOLINESS POSSIBLE IN THE NATURAL STATE.*

### DIRECTION.

We cannot attain to the Practice of true Holiness by any of our endeavours while we continue in *our Natural State*, and are not partakers of a New State by union and fellowship with Christ through faith.

HERE ariseth the consideration of two states or conditions of the children of men in matters that appertain to God and godliness, the one of which is vastly different from the other. Those that have the happiness of a new birth and creation in Christ by faith are thereby placed in a very excellent state, consisting in the enjoyment of the righteousness of Christ for their justification, and of the Spirit of Christ to live by, in holiness here, and in glory hereafter for ever, as hath already appeared. Those that are not in Christ by faith cannot be in a better state than that which they received together with their nature from the first Adam, by being once born and created in him, or than they can attain to by the power of that nature with any such help as God is pleased to afford to it.

It is positively asserted by the Apostle Paul, "that those that are in the flesh cannot please God" (Rom. viii. 8). Many are too overly and negligent in considering the sense of this gospel-phrase—what it is to be in the flesh. They understand no more by it than to be sinful, or to be addicted inordinately to please the sensitive appetite. They should consider that the apostle speaketh here of " being in the flesh " as the cause of sinfulness, as in the next verse he speaketh of " being in the Spirit " as the cause of holiness ; and, whatever cause it be, it must needs be distinct from its effect. Sin is a property of the flesh, or something that dwelleth in the flesh (Rom. vii. 18), and therefore it is not the flesh itself. The flesh is that " which lusteth against the Spirit " (Gal. v. 17), and therefore it is not merely sinful lusting. The true interpretation is, that by *flesh* is meant the nature of man, as it is corrupted by the fall of Adam, and propagated from him to us in that corrupt state by natural generation ; and " to be in the flesh " is to be in a natural state, as " to be in the Spirit " is to be in a new state, by the Spirit of Christ dwelling in us (Rom. viii. 9). The corrupt nature is called " flesh," because it is received by *carnal* generation ; and the new nature is called " Spirit," because it is received by *spiritual* regeneration. " That which is born of the flesh is flesh ; and that which is born of the Spirit is spirit " (John iii. 6). So the apostle, if he be rightly understood, hath said enough to make us despair utterly of attaining to true holiness, while we continue in a natural state.

The apostle testifieth, that those who have been taught as the truth is in Jesus, have learned to avoid the former sinful conversation, by putting off the old man, which is corrupt according to the deceitful lusts ; and by putting on the new man, which, after God, is created in righteousness and true holiness (Eph. iv. 21, 22, 24). " Putting off the old man," and " putting on the new man," is the same thing with " not being in the flesh, but in the Spirit," in the foregoing testimony—that is, putting off our natural state and putting on a new state by union and fellowship with Christ. The apostle himself showeth, that by " the new man " is meant that excellent state where " Christ is all, and in all " (Col. iii. 11). Therefore, by " the old man " must needs be meant the natural state of man, wherein

he is without the saving enjoyment of Christ; which is
called old, because of the new state to which believers are
brought by their regeneration in Christ. This is a manner
of expression peculiar to the gospel, as well as the former,
and as slightly considered by those that think that the
apostle's meaning is only that they should put off sinfulness and put on holiness in their conversation; and so
they think to become new men by turning over a new leaf
in their practice, and leading a new life. Let them learn
here that the old and new man are two contrary states,
containing in them not only sin and holiness, but all other
things that dispose and incline us to the practice of them;
and that the old man must be put off, as crucified with
Christ, before we can be freed from the practice of sin
(Rom. vi. 6, 7). And therefore we cannot lead a new
life until we have first gotten a new state by faith in
Christ.

## CHAPTER VI.

### *NO HOLINESS NEEDED TO GIVE A TITLE TO CHRIST.*

---

### DIRECTION.

Those that endeavour to perform sincere obedience to all the commands of Christ, *as the condition whereby they are to procure for themselves a right and title to salvation,* and a good ground to trust on Him for the same, do seek their salvation by the works of the law, and not by the faith of Christ as He is revealed in the Gospel: and they shall never be able to perform sincerely any true holy obedience by all such endeavours.

THE difference between the law and gospel doth not at all consist in this, that the one requireth *perfect* doing, the other only *sincere* doing; but in this, that the one requireth *doing,* the other, *no doing* but *believing* for life and salvation.  Their terms are different, not only in degree, but in their whole nature. If we seek salvation by never so easy and mild a condition of works, we do thereby bring ourselves under the terms of the law, and do become debtors to fulfil the whole law in perfection, though we intended to engage ourselves only to fulfil it in part (Gal. v. 3); for the law is a complete declaration of the only terms whereby God will judge all that are not brought to despair of procuring salvation by any of their own works, and to receive it as a gift freely given to them by the grace of God in Christ.

The end which God aimed at in giving the law to Moses, was not that any should ever attain to holiness or salvation by the condition of perfect or sincere obedience to it; though, if there had been any such way of salvation at that time, it must have consisted in the performance of that law which was then given to the Church to be a rule of life, as well as a covenant. There was another covenant made before that time with Abraham, Isaac, and Jacob—a covenant of grace, promising all blessings freely through Christ, the promised Seed, by which only they were to be saved. And the covenant of the law was added that they might see their sinfulness and subjection to death and wrath, and the impossibility of attaining to life or holiness by their works, and be forced to trust on the free promise only for all their salvation, and that sin might be restrained by the spirit of bondage, until the coming of that promised seed Jesus Christ, and the more plentiful pouring out of the sanctifying Spirit by Him. This the Apostle Paul showeth largely (Gal. iii. 15–24; Rom. v. 20, 21, and x. 3, 4). None of the Israelites under the Old Testament were ever saved by the Sinai covenant; neither did any of them ever attain to holiness by the terms of it. Some of them did indeed perform the commandments of it sincerely, though imperfectly : but those were first justified and made partakers of life and holiness by virtue of that better covenant made with Abraham, Isaac, and Jacob, which was the same in substance with the new covenant or testament established by the blood of Christ. Had it not been for that better covenant, the Sinai covenant would have proved to them an occasion of no happiness, but only of sin, despair, and destruction.

# CHAPTER VII.

## NO HOLINESS NEEDED AS A PREPARATION FOR BELIEVING IN CHRIST.

---

### DIRECTION.

We are not to Imagine that *our Hearts and Lives must be changed* from Sin to Holiness in any Measure *before we may safely venture to trust* on Christ for the Sure Enjoyment of Himself and His Salvation.

WE are naturally so prone to ground our salvation upon our own works, that, if we cannot make them *procuring conditions and causes* of our salvation by Christ, yet we shall endeavour at least to make them *necessary preparatives to fit us* for receiving Christ and His salvation by faith. And men are easily persuaded that this is not at all contrary to salvation by free grace, because all that is hereby ascribed to our works, or good qualifications, is only that they put us in a fit posture to receive a free gift. If we were to go to a prince for a free gift, good manners and due reverence would teach us to trim ourselves first, and to change our slovenly clothes, as Joseph did when he came out of the dungeon into the presence of Pharaoh. It seemeth to be an impudent slighting and contemning the justice and holiness of God and Christ, and an unsufferable affront and indignity offered to the divine Majesty, when any dare presume to approach His presence in the nasty pickle of his sins, covered all over with putrefying sores, not at all closed. bound up, or cleansed.

Any the least change of our hearts and lives from sin to holiness before our receiving of Christ and His salvation by faith, is not at all necessary according to the terms of the gospel, nor required in the word of God. Christ would have the vilest sinners come to Him for salvation immediately, without delaying the time to prepare themselves for Him. Christ would have us to believe on Him that justifieth the ungodly; and therefore He doth not require us to be godly before we believe (Rom. iv. 5). Therefore it is no affront to Christ, or slighting and contemning the justice and holiness of God, to come to Christ while we are polluted sinners; but rather it is an affronting and contemning the saving grace, merit, and fulness of Christ, if we endeavour to make ourselves righteous and holy before we receive Christ Himself, and all righteousness and holiness in Him by faith.

He is a saving Lord; trust on Him first to save you from the guilt and power of sin, and dominion of Satan, and to give you a new spiritual disposition; then, and not till then, the love of Christ will constrain you to resign yourself heartily to live to Him that died for you (2 Cor. v. 14), and you will be able to say with an unfeigned resolution, "O Lord, truly I am Thy servant; I am Thy servant, and the son of Thine handmaid: Thou hast loosed my bonds" (Ps. cxvi. 16).

Act faith first, and the apprehension of God's love to thy soul will sweetly allure and constrain thee to love God and His service universally: "We love Him, because He first loved us" (1 John iv. 19). We cannot be beforehand with God in love; and we must perceive His love, to make us love Him. The first right holy thoughts thou canst have of God are thoughts of His grace and mercy to thy soul in Christ, which are included in the grace of faith. Get these thoughts first by believing in Christ, and they will breed in thee love to God and all good thoughts of Him. Godly sorrow for sin is wrought in us by believing the pardoning grace of God; as it is found by experience that a pardon from a prince will sometimes sooner draw tears from a stubborn malefactor than the fear of a halter will. Thus the sinful woman was brought to wash Christ's feet with her tears (Luke vii. 37, 38). We are not like to be sorry for grieving God with our sins, while we look upon Him as an enemy that will ease Himself well enough of His burden, and right Himself upon us by our everlasting destruction. The belief of God's pardoning and accepting grace is a necessary means to bring us to an ingenuous confession of sins. The people freely confessed their sins, when they were baptized of John in Jordan, for the remission of sins (Mark i. 4, 5). The confession of despairers is forced, like the extorted confessions and cryings out of malefactors upon the rack. A pardon sooner openeth the mouth to an ingenuous confession than " Confess and be hanged," or " Confess and be damned." Therefore, if you would freely confess your sins, believe, first, that " God is faithful and just to forgive your sins " through Christ (1 John i. 9).

# CHAPTER VIII.

*NO HOLINESS BUT IN UNION WITH CHRIST.*

——

### DIRECTION.

Be sure to seek for *Holiness* of Heart and Life only in its due order, where God hath placed it, *after union with Christ,* justification, and the gift of the Holy Ghost; and, in that order, seek it earnestly by faith, as a very necessary part of your salvation.

It is a matter of high concern to be acquainted with the due place and order wherein God hath settled this holy practice in the mystery of our salvation, and a great point of Christian wisdom to seek it only in that order. We know that God is the God of order, and that His infinite wisdom hath appeared in appointing the order of His creatures, which order we are forced to observe for the attainment of our ends in worldly things; so likewise in spiritual things "God hath made an everlasting covenant, ordered in all things, and sure" (2 Sam. xxiii. 5). The benefits of it have an orderly dependence each upon other, as links of the same golden chain, though several of them, and a *title* to all of them, are given to us at one and the same time. And I think enough hath been said already to show in what order God brings us to the practice of the moral law. He first maketh us to be in Christ by faith, as branches in the vine, that we may bring forth much fruit (John xv. 4, 5). He first purgeth our consciences from dead works by justification, that we may serve the living God (Heb. ix. 14). He first maketh us to live in the Spirit, and then to walk in the Spirit (Gal. v. 25). This is the order prescribed in the gospel, which is "the power of God unto salvation."

Now, mark well the great advantages you have for the attainment of holiness, by seeking it in a right gospel order. You will have the advantage of the love of God manifested toward you, in forgiving your sins, receiving you into favour, and giving you the Spirit of adoption, and the hope of His glory, freely through Christ, to persuade and constrain you by sweet allurements to love God again, who hath so dearly loved you, and to love others for His sake, and to give up yourselves to the obedience of all His commands out of a hearty love to Him: you will also enjoy the help of the Spirit of God, to incline you powerfully unto obedience, and to strengthen you for the performance of it against all your corruptions and the temptations of Satan; so that you will have both wind and tide to forward your voyage in the practice of holiness.

Oh that people would be persuaded to consider the due place of holiness in the mystery of salvation, and to seek it only there, where they have all the advantage of gospel-grace to find it!

We are to look upon holiness as a very necessary part of that salvation that is received by faith in Christ. Though salvation be often taken in Scripture, by way of eminency, for its perfection in the state of heavenly glory, yet, according to its full and proper signification, we are to understand by it all that freedom from the evil of our natural corrupt state, and all those holy and happy enjoyments that we receive from Christ our Saviour, either in this world by faith, or in the world to come by glorification. Holiness in this life is absolutely necessary to salvation, not only as a means to the end, but by a nobler kind of necessity, as part of the end itself. Though we are not saved by good works as procuring causes, yet we ——— ———-¹ to good works, as fruits and effects of saving grace, " which God hath prepared that we should walk in them" (Eph. ii. 10).

Holiness of heart and life is to be sought for earnestly by faith as a very necessary part of our salvation. Great multitudes of ignorant people that live under the gospel harden their hearts in sin, and ruin their souls for ever, by trusting on Christ for such an imaginary salvation, as consisteth not at all in holiness, but only in forgiveness of sin and deliverance from everlasting torments.

The way to oppose this pernicious delusion is, not to deny, as some do, that trusting on Christ for salvation is a saving act of faith, but rather to show that none do or can trust on Christ for true salvation except they trust on Him for holiness; neither do they heartily desire true salvation if they do not desire to be made holy and righteous in their hearts and lives. If ever God and Christ gave you salvation, holiness will be one part of it; if Christ wash you not from the filth of your sins, you have no part with Him (John xiii. 8). What a strange kind of salvation do they desire that care not for holiness! They would be saved *by* Christ, and yet be *out* of Christ in a fleshly state.

True gospel-faith maketh us come to Christ with a thirsty appetite that we may drink of living water, even of His sanctifying Spirit (John viii. 37, 38), and cry out earnestly to Him to save us, not only from hell but from sin, saying, " Teach us to do Thy will; Thy Spirit is good" (Ps. cxliii. 10); " Turn Thou me, and I shall be turned" (Jer. xxxi. 18); " Create in me a clean heart, O God, and renew a right spirit within me" (Ps. li. 10). This is the way whereby the doctrine of salvation by grace doth necessitate us to holiness of life, by constraining us to seek for it by faith in Christ, as a substantial part of that salvation which is freely given to us through Christ.

# CHAPTER IX.

### NO HOLINESS WITHOUT FIRST ACCEPTING THE COMFORTS OF THE GOSPEL.

---

### DIRECTION.

We must *first* receive *the comforts of the Gospel* that we may be able to perform sincerely the duties of the Law.

WE are by nature so strongly addicted to the legal method of salvation, that it is a hard matter to dissuade those that live under the light of the gospel from placing the *duties* of the law *before the comforts* of the gospel. If they cannot make salvation itself, yet they will be sure to make all the comforts of it to depend upon their own works.

They think it as unreasonable to expect comfort before duty, as wages before work, or the fruits of the earth before the husbandman's labour (2 Tim. ii. 6).

The usual method of gospel doctrine, as it is delivered to us in the Holy Scripture, is first to comfort our hearts, and thereby to establish us in every good word and work (2 Thess. ii. 17). And this method appears most clearly adjusted in several epistles written by the apostles, wherein they first acquaint the churches with the rich grace of God towards them in Christ, and the spiritual blessings which they are made partakers of, for their strong consolation; and then they exhort them to an holy conversation answerable to such privileges. And it is not only the method of whole epistles, but of many particular exhortations to duty, wherein the comfortable benefits of the grace of God in Christ are made use of as arguments and motives to stir up the saints to a holy practice ; which comfortable benefits must first be believed, and the comfort of them applied to our own souls, or else they will not be forcible to engage us to the practice for which they are intended. To give you a few instances of a multitude that might be alleged : we are exhorted to practice holy duties, because we are dead to sin and alive to God through Jesus Christ our Lord (Rom. vi. 11); because sin shall not have dominion over us; for we are not under the law, but under grace (Rom. vi. 14); because we are not in the flesh but in the Spirit; and God will quicken our mortal bodies by His Spirit dwelling in us (Rom. viii. 9, 11); because our bodies are the members of Christ, and the temples of the Holy Ghost (1 Cor. vi. 15, 19).

We may require a strong healthy person first to work, and then to expect meat, drink, and wages ; but a fainting, famished person must first have food, or a reviving cordial, to strengthen his heart, before he can work.

Both Scripture and experience show that this is the method whereby God bringeth His people from sin to holiness. Though some of them are brought under terrors for a while, that sin may be the more embittered, and the salvation of Christ rendered more precious and acceptable to them, yet such are again delivered from their terrors by the comfort of God's salvation, that they may be fitted for holiness. And generally a holy life beginneth with comfort, and is maintained by it.

I dare appeal to the experience of any that obey God out of hearty love. Let them examine themselves, and consider, whether they were brought to give up themselves to serve God in love, without comfortable apprehensions of the love of God towards them? I dare affirm, without fear of contradiction, there are no such prodigies in the new birth.

## CHAPTER X.

### *NO HOLINESS WITHOUT SOME MEASURE OF ASSURANCE.*

### DIRECTION.

That we may be prepared by the comforts of the Gospel to perform sincerely the duties of the Law, we must get some
*Assurance of our Salvation*, in that very Faith whereby
Christ Himself is received into our hearts : therefore we
must endeavour to Believe on Christ confidently, persuading and assuring ourselves, in the Act of Believing, that
God freely giveth to us an interest in Christ and His Salvation according to His Gracious Promise.

It is evident that those comforts of the gospel that are
necessary to an holy practice, cannot be truly received
without some assurance of our interest in Christ and His
salvation. Hence it will clearly follow that this assurance
is very necessary to enable us for the practice of holiness,
as those comforts must go before the duties of the law in
order of nature, as the cause goeth before the effect, though
not in any distance of time. My present work is to show
what this assurance is, that is so necessary unto holiness,
and which I have here asserted we must act in that very
faith whereby we receive Christ Himself into our hearts,
even in justifying saving faith.

It is a great and necessary office of saving faith to
purify the heart, and to enable us to live and walk in

the practice of all holy duties, by the grace of Christ, and by Christ Himself living in us, as hath been showed before; which office faith is not able to perform, except some assurance of our own interest in Christ and His salvation be comprehended in the nature of it. If we would live to God, not to ourselves, by Christ living in us, according to Paul's example, we must be able to assure ourselves as he did, " Christ loved me, and gave Himself for me " (Gal. ii. 20). We are taught, that, "if we live in the Spirit, we should walk in the Spirit " (Gal. v. 25). It would be high presumption if we should endeavour to walk above our natural strength and power by the Spirit, before we have made sure of our living by the Spirit. I have showed, that we cannot make use of the comfortable benefits of the saving grace of Christ, whereby the gospel doth engage and encourage us to an holy practice, except we have some confidence of our own interest in those saving benefits. If we do not assuredly believe that we are dead to sin, and alive to God through Christ, and risen with Christ, and not under the law, but under grace, and members of Christ's body, the temple of His Spirit, the dear children of God, it would be hypocrisy to serve God upon the account of such privileges, as if we reckoned ourselves to be partakers of them.

No other faith will work by love, and therefore will not avail to salvation in Christ (Gal. v. 6). The Apostle James putteth thee upon showing thy faith by thy works (Jas. ii. 18). And, in this trial, this faith of assurance cometh off with high praise and honour. When God called His people to work outward miracles by it, all things have been possible to them; and it hath frequently brought forth such works of righteousness, as may be deservedly esteemed great spiritual miracles. From hence hath proceeded that heroic fortitude of the people of God, whereby their absolute obedience to God hath shined forth in doing and suffering those great things which are recorded in the Holy Scriptures, and in the histories of the Church.

# CHAPTER XI.

## THE DUTY OF BELIEVING.

### DIRECTION.

Endeavour diligently to perform *the great work of believing on Christ, in a right manner, without any delay, and then also to continue and increase in your most holy faith;* that so your enjoyment of Christ, union and fellowship with Him, and all holiness by Him, may be begun, continued, and increased in you.

HAVING already discovered to you the powerful and effectual means of an holy practice, my remaining work is to lead you to the actual exercise and improvement of them for the immediate attainment of the end. And I think it may be clearly perceived by the foregoing directions, that faith in Christ is the duty with which a holy life is to begin, and by which the foundation of all other holy duties is laid in the soul. It is before sufficiently proved that Christ Himself, with all endowments necessary to enable us to an holy practice, is received actually into our hearts by faith. This is the uniting grace whereby the Spirit of God knitteth the knot of mystical marriage between Christ and us, and maketh us branches of that noble vine, members of that body, joined to that excellent head, living stones of the spiritual temple, built upon the precious living corner stone and sure foundation; partakers of the bread and drink that came down from heaven, and giveth life to the world. If we put the question,

" What must we do, that we may work the works of God?" Christ resolveth it, "That we believe on Him whom He hath sent" (John vi. 28, 29). He putteth us first upon the work of believing which is *the* work of God by way of eminency, the work of works, because all other good works proceed from it.

The FIRST thing in the present direction is to put you upon the performance of this great work of believing on Christ, and to guide you therein. You are to make it your diligent endeavour to perform the great work of believing on Christ.

We must labour to enter into that rest, lest any man fall by unbelief (Heb iv. 11). "We must show diligence to the full assurance of hope to the end, that we may be followers of them who through faith and patience inherit the promises" (Heb. vi. 11, 12). It is a work that requireth the exercise of might and power; and therefore we have need to be strengthened with might by the Spirit in the inward man, that Christ may dwell in our hearts by faith (Eph. iii. 16, 17). I confess it is easy, pleasant, and delicious in its own nature, because it is a motion of the heart without any cumbersome bodily labour; and it is a taking Christ and His salvation as our own, which is very comfortable and delightful; and the soul is carried forth in this by love to Christ and its own happiness, which is an affection that maketh even hard works easy and pleasant; yet it is made difficult to us by reason of the opposition that it meets with from our own inward corruptions, and from Satan's temptations.

Though we cannot possibly perform this great work in a right manner, until the Spirit of God work faith in our hearts by His mighty power, yet it is necessary that we should endeavour it, and that too before we can find the Spirit of God working faith effectually in us, or giving strength to believe. The way whereby the Spirit works faith in the elect is, by stirring them up to endeavour to believe. Neither can we possibly find that the Spirit of God doth effectually work faith or give strength to believe, until we act it; for all inward graces, as well as all other inward habits, are discerned by their acts, as seed in the ground by its springing. We cannot see any such thing as love to God or man in our hearts before we act it. Children know not their ability to stand upon their feet until they have made trial, by endeavouring so to do; so we know not our spiritual strength until we have learned by experience from the use and exercise of it. Therefore, as soon as we know the duty of believing, we are to apply ourselves immediately to the vigorous performance of the duty, and in so doing, we shall find that the Spirit of Christ hath strengthened us to believe, though we know not certainly beforehand that He will do it.

The SECOND thing directed to is, that you should endeavour for a right *manner* of performing this duty. This is a point of great concernment, because the want of it will render your faith ineffectual to sanctification and salvation. The great duty of love, which is the end of the law and the principal fruit of sanctification, must flow from faith unfeigned (1 Tim. i. 5).

I have given you before, in this treatise, a description of saving faith, and have showed that it containeth two acts in it; the one is, believing the truth of the gospel; the other is, believing on Christ, as revealed and freely promised to us in the gospel for all His salvation. Now, your great endeavour must be, to perform both these acts in a right manner; as I shall show concerning each of them in particular.

In the *first* place, you are highly concerned to endeavour for a right belief of the truth of the gospel of Christ; that so you may be well furnished, disposed, and encouraged to believe on Christ, as revealed and promised in the gospel. You are to believe assuredly that there is no way to be saved, without receiving *all* the saving benefits of Christ, His Spirit as well as His merits, sanctification as well as remission of sins, by faith. It is the ruin of many souls, that they trust on Christ for remission of sins, without any regard to holiness; whereas these two great benefits, forgiveness and holiness, are inseparably joined in Christ, so that none are freed from condemnation by Christ, but those that are enabled to walk holily—*i.e.*, not after the flesh, but after the Spirit (Rom. viii. 1). It is also the ruin of many other souls that they seek remission of sins by faith in Christ, and look for holiness not by faith, but in another way—viz., by their own endeavours according to the terms of the law; whereas we can never live to God in holiness, except we be dead to the law, and live only by ·Christ living in us by faith. That faith which receiveth not holiness as well as remission of sins from Christ will never sanctify us, and therefore it will never bring us to heavenly glory (Heb. xii. 14).

You are to be fully persuaded of the truth of the general free promise in your own particular case, that if you believe on Christ sincerely you shall have everlasting life, as well as any other in the world, without performing any condition of works to procure an interest in Christ; for the promise "Whosoever believeth on Him shall not be ashamed" (Rom. ix. 33), is universal, without any exception.

You are to believe assuredly that it is the will of God that you, as well as any other, should believe in Christ, and have eternal life by Him; and that your believing is a duty very acceptable to God; and that He will help you, as well as any other, in this work, because He calleth and commandeth you by the gospel to believe in Christ. This maketh us to set cheerfully upon the work of believing; as when Jesus commanded the blind man to be called, they said unto him, "Be of good comfort, rise; He calleth thee" (Mark x. 49). A command of Christ made Peter walk upon the water (Matt. xiv. 29). And here we are not to meddle with God's secret of predestination, or the purpose of His will to give the grace of faith to some rather than to others; but only with His revealed will, in His gracious invitations and commands, by which we are required to believe on Christ.

I come now to the *second* principal act of faith, where-

by Christ Himself, and His Spirit, and all His saving
benefits, are actually received into the heart, which is
believing on Christ as revealed and freely promised to us
in the gospel for all His salvation. The Spirit of God
doth habitually dispose and incline our hearts to a right
performance of this act by enabling us to perform the
first act, according to the former instructions in believing
assuredly those great things of the gospel whereby we are
delivered into a form of doctrine (Rom. vi. 17, *margin*);
and this form of doctrine we are to obey from our hearts,
and to follow as our pattern in the manner of our acting
faith in Christ for salvation. Therefore I need only exhort you briefly to act your faith in Christ, according to
that form and pattern in which we have been already so
largely instructed. You are to believe in Christ as alone
sufficient, and all-sufficient for your happiness and salvation.

You are also to receive Christ merely as a free gift
given to the chief of sinners, resolving that you will not
perform any conditions to procure yourselves a right and
title to Him, but that you will come to Him as a lost
sinner, an ungodly creature, trusting on Him that justifieth the ungodly.

Another thing to be observed diligently is, that you
must come to Christ for a new holy heart and life, and
all things necessary thereunto, as well as for deliverance
from the wrath of God, and the torments of hell.

The *third* thing contained in this direction is, the
avoiding *all delay* in the performance of this great work
of believing in Christ. We should make haste, and not
delay, to keep God's commandments (Ps. cxix. 60); and
fly for refuge to the hope set before us (Heb. vi. 18).
And God commanded us to fly thus by faith, without
which it is impossible to please God in other duties.
The work is of such a nature that it may be performed
as soon as you hear the gospel: "As soon as they hear of
me, they shall obey me" (Ps. xviii. 44). "As soon as Zion
travailed, she brought forth her children" (Isa. lxvi. 8).

Some imagine that, after they have heard the gospel of salvation by Christ, they may lawfully defer the believing it until they have sufficiently examined the truth of some other different doctrine, or until God be pleased to afford them some other means to assure them fully of the truth of the gospel. Thus, they that are called Seekers misspend the day of grace, ever learning, but never coming to the knowledge of the truth (2 Tim. iii. 7).

Another sort of people there are that delay the great work of believing, to the ruin of their souls, resting in an attendance upon the outward means of grace and salvation, instead of any endeavours to receive Christ by faith, though they be convinced of the truth of the gospel. This they call waiting upon God at the doors of His grace and salvation, in the use of means appointed by Him, and sitting under the droppings of the sanctuary. But let them know that this is not the right waiting on God required in the Scripture. It is rather disobedience to God, and to the means of His appointment, who requires that we should be doers of the Word, and not hearers only, deceiving ourselves (Jas. i. 22).

What is it that these deluded ones wait for before they perform the duty of believing? Is it for more knowledge of the gospel? The way to increase thy knowledge, as well as any other talent, is to make use of what thou hast received already. Believe heartily on Christ for all thy salvation, according to that little knowledge of the gospel which thou hast, and thou wilt have an interest in the promise of knowledge contained in the new covenant: "They shall all know me, from the least to the greatest of them, saith the Lord" (Jer. xxxi. 34). Dost thou wait for any manifestations or flowings in of God's saving love to thy soul? Then the way to obtain it is to believe, that so the God of hope may fill thee with all joy and peace in believing (Rom. xv. 13). Thou hast sufficient manifestation of God's love to thy soul by the free promises of life and salvation by Christ. Do but trust on the name of the Lord, and stay upon thy God, when thou walkest

D

in darkest, and seest no light of sensible comforts any other way; otherwise thou waitest for comfort in vain, and this shalt thou have at the Lord's hand, thou shalt lie down in sorrow (Isa. l. 10, 11). Dost thou wait for any qualifications to prepare thee for the work of believing? If they be good and holy qualifications thou canst not have them *before* faith; but they are either included in the nature of faith, or they are fruits of it, as hath already been largely proved.

The FOURTH thing in the direction is, that we should *continue* and *increase* in this most holy faith. And, that we may, we must not think that, when we have once attained to the grace of saving faith, and thereby are begotten anew in Christ, our names are up in heaven, and therefore we may be careless; but as long as we continue in this life we must endeavour to continue in the faith, grounded and settled, not moved away from the hope of the gospel (Col. i. 23); and to hold the beginning of our confidence, and the rejoicing of hope, steadfast to the end (Heb. iii. 6, 14); and to build up ourselves in our most holy faith (Jude, ver. 20), abounding therein with thanksgiving (Col. ii. 7). Though we receive Christ freely by faith, yet we are but babes in Christ (1 Cor. iii. 1). And we must not account that we have already attained, or are already perfect (Phil. iii. 12, 13); but we must strive to be more rooted and built up in Him, until we come unto a perfect man, unto the measure of the stature of the fulness of Christ (Eph. iv. 13). If the new nature be really in us by regeneration it will, as the new-born babe, have an appetite to its own continuance and increase, until it come to perfection (1 Pet. ii. 2).  And we are not only to receive Christ and a new holy nature by faith, but also to live and walk by it, and to resist the devil, and to quench all his fiery darts by it, and also to grow in grace, and to perfect holiness in the fear of God; for we are kept by the mighty power of God through faith unto salvation (1 Pet. i. 5). As all our Christian warfare is the good fight of faith (1 Tim. vi. 12), so *all spiritual life* and holiness continues, grows, or decays in us, *according as faith continueth, groweth, or decayeth in vigour;* but, when this faith beginneth to sink by fears and doubtings, the man himself beginneth to sink together with it (Matt. xiv. 29–31). Faith is like the hand of Moses; while it is held up, Israel prevails; while it is let down, Amalek prevails (Exod. xvii. 11).

If you do not find that your believing in such a right manner as I have described doth produce such fruits of holiness as you desire, you ought not to diminish, but rather to increase, your confidence in Christ, knowing that the weakness of your faith hindereth its fruitfulness; and the greater your confidence is concerning the love of God to you in Christ, the greater will be your love to God and to His service. If you fall into any gross sin after the work is began in you, as David and Peter did, think not that you must cast away your confidence, and expect nothing but wrath from God and Christ, and that you must refuse to be comforted by the grace of Christ, at least for some time; for thus you would be more weak, and prone to fall into other sins; but rather strive still to trust more confidently, seeing you have an Advocate with the Father, Jesus Christ the righteous, and that He is the propitiation for our sins (1 John ii. 1, 2). And let not the guilt of sin stay *at all* upon your conscience, but wash it away with all speed in the fountain of Christ's blood, which is opened for us that it may be ready for our use on all such incident occasions. Strive to keep and to increase faith by faith—*i.e.*, by acting faith, frequently, by trusting on God to keep and increase it, being confident "that He which hath began a good work in you will perform it until the day of Jesus Christ" (Phil. i. 6); and saying with the Psalmist, "The Lord will perfect that which concerneth me" (Psalm cxxxviii. 8).

# CHAPTER XII.

## *HOLINESS THROUGH FAITH.*

---

### DIRECTION.

*Make diligent use of your most Holy Faith, for the immediate performance of the duties of the Law,* by walking no longer according to your old natural State, or any Principles or Means of Practice that belong unto it, but *only according to that new State which you receive by Faith,* and the Principles and Means of Practice that properly belong thereunto, and strive to continue and increase in such manner of practice. This is the only way to attain to an acceptable performance of these Holy and Righteous Duties, as far as it is possible, in this present life.

HERE I am guiding you to *the manner of practice,* wherein you are to make use of faith, and of all other effectual means of holiness before treated of, which faith layeth hold on, for the immediate performance of the law; which is the great end aimed at in this whole treatise. And therefore this deserveth to be diligently considered, as the principal direction, to which all the foregoing and following are subservient. As for the meaning of it, I have already showed that our old natural state is that which we derive from the first Adam by natural generation, and it is called in the Scripture "the old man;" and while we be in it we are said to be "in the flesh." And our new state is that which we receive from the second Adam, Jesus Christ, by being new born in union and fellowship with Him through faith, and it is called in Scripture "the

new man ; " and when we are in it we are said to be " in
the Spirit."

The principles and means of practice belonging to a
natural state are such as persons do, or may attain and
make use of, before they are in Christ by faith. Such as
belong properly to the new state, are the manifold holy
endowments, privileges, and enjoyments, which we partake
of in Christ by faith, such as have already appeared to be
the only effectual means of a holy life. We are said to
walk according to either of these states, or to the principles
or means that belong to either of them, when we are
moved and guided by virtue of them to such actings as
are agreeable to them. The manner of the practice here
directed to consists in moving and guiding ourselves in the
performance of the works of the law by gospel principles and
means. This is the rare and excellent art of godliness, in
which every Christian should strive to be skilful and expert.
The reason why many come off with shame and confusion,
after they have a long time laboured with much zeal and
industry for the attainment of true godliness, is because
they were never acquainted with this holy art, and never
endeavoured to practise it in a right gospel way.

It is a manner of practice far above the sphere of natural
ability, such as would never have entered into the hearts
of the wisest in the world, if it had not been revealed to
us in the Scriptures. And when it is there most plainly
revealed, continueth a dark riddle to those that are not in-
wardly enlightened and taught by the Holy Spirit. Such
as many godly persons, guided by the Spirit, do in some
measure walk in, yet do but obscurely discern ; they can
hardly perceive their own knowledge of it, and can hardly
give any account to others of the way wherein they walk,
as the disciples that walked in Christ the way to the
Father, and yet perceived not that knowledge in themselves: "Lord, we know not whither Thou goest, and how
can we know the way ?" (John xiv. 5). *This is the reason
why many poor believers are so weak in Christ,* and attain
so small a degree of holiness and righteousness. There-

fore, that you may the better be acquainted with a mystery of so high concernment, I shall show, in the first place, that the Holy Scriptures do direct you to this manner of practice, as only effectual for the performance of holy duties; and then I shall lay before you some necessary instructions, that you may understand how to walk aright in it; and continue and go forward therein till you be made perfect in Christ.

For the FIRST of these the Holy Scriptures are very large and clear in directing us to this manner of practice, and to continuance and growth therein.

1. This is the manner of practice in Scripture, which is expressed by "living by faith" (Hab. ii. 4; Gal. ii. 20; Heb. x. 38), "walking by faith" (2 Cor. v. 7), "faith working by love" (Gal. v. 6), "overcoming the world by faith" (1 John v. 4), "quenching all the fiery darts of the wicked by the shield of faith" (Eph. vi. 16). Some make no more of living and walking by faith than merely a stirring-up and encouraging ourselves to our duty by such principles as we believe. But if this was all that was intended by these expressions, then the Jews might account that they lived by faith, because they professed and assented unto the doctrine of Moses and the Prophets, and were moved thereby to a zeal of God; yet we are expressly told of them, that they sought righteousness not by faith, but as it were by the works of the law (Rom. ix. 32). As it is one and the same thing to be justified by faith, and by Christ believed on (Rom. v. 1), so to live, walk, and work by faith is all one with living, walking, working by means of Christ and His saving endowments, which we receive and make use of by faith, to guide and move ourselves to the practice of holiness.

2. The same thing is commended to us by the terms of "walking in Christ," "rooted and built up in Him" (Col. ii. 6, 7), "living to God and not to ourselves, but to have Christ living in us" (Gal. ii. 19, 20), "good conversation in Christ" (1 Pet. iii. 16), "putting on the Lord Jesus Christ, that we may walk honestly as in the day" (Rom.

xiii. 13, 14), "being strong in the Lord, and in the power
of His might" (Eph. vi. 10), "doing all things in the
name of Christ" (Col. iii. 17), "walking up and down in
the name of the Lord " (Zech. x. 12), "going in the
strength of the Lord, making mention of His righteousness, even of His only" (Ps. lxxi. 16). These phrases are
frequent, and do sufficiently explain one another, and do
show that we are to practice holiness, not only by virtue
of Christ's authority, but also of His strengthening endowments moving us and encouraging us thereunto.

3. It is also signified by the phrases of "being strong in
the grace that is in Christ Jesus" (2 Tim. ii. 1), "having
our conversation in the world, not with fleshly wisdom,
but by the grace of God" (2 Cor. i. 12), " having or holding fast grace, that we may serve God acceptably " (Heb.
xii. 28), "labouring abundantly," in such a manner as that
the whole work is not performed by us but "by the grace
of God that is with us" (1 Cor. xv. 10). By grace,
therefore, we may well understand the privileges of our
new state given to us in Christ, whereby we ought to be
influenced and guided in the performance of holy duties.

4. It is also signified, when we are taught " to put off
the old and put on the new man ; " yea, to continue in so
doing, though we have done it in a measure already (Eph.
iv. 21, 22, 24), and to avoid sin, "because we have put
off the old and put on the new man" (Col. iii. 9, 10). I
have already showed that by this twofold man is not
meant merely sin and holiness ; but by the former is meant
our natural state, with all its endowments, whereby we are
furnished only to the practice of sin, and by the latter our
new state in Christ, whereby we are furnished with all
means necessary for the practice of holiness.

5. We are to understand the same thing when we are
taught "not to walk after the flesh, but after the Spirit,
that we may be free from the law of sin, and that the
righteousness of the law may be fulfilled in us" (Rom.
viii. 1-4) ; and "through the Spirit to mortify the deeds
of the body" (Rom. viii. 13) ; and "to be led by the

Spirit, because we live by the Spirit, and have crucified the flesh with the affections and lusts " (Gal. v. 24). The apostle doth show by these expressions not only that we are to practice holiness, but also by what means we may do it effectually. By " the flesh " is meant our old nature, derived from the first Adam ; and by " the Spirit " is meant the Spirit of Christ, and that new nature which we have by Him dwelling in us. We are said to walk after either of these natures, when we make the properties or qualifications of either of them to be the principles of our practice. So when we are taught " to serve in newness of spirit, and not in the oldness of the letter, that so we may bring forth fruit unto God," the meaning is, that we must endeavour to bring forth the fruits of holiness, not by virtue of the law, that killing letter to which the flesh is married, and by which the motions of sin are in us, but by virtue of the Spirit and His manifold riches, which we partake of in our new state, by a mystical marriage with Christ (Rom. vii. 4-6), and by virtue of such principles as belong to the new state declared in the gospel, whereby the Holy Spirit is ministered to us.

6. This is the manner of walking which the apostle Paul directeth us unto, when he teacheth us by his own example that the continual work of our lives should be " to know Christ, and the power of His resurrection, and the fellowship of His sufferings, being made conformable to His death ; if by any means we may attain unto the resurrection of the dead, and to increase and press forward in this kind of knowledge " (Phil. iii. 10-12, 14). Certainly he meaneth such an experimental knowledge of Christ, and of His death and resurrection, as effectually makes us conformable thereunto, in dying unto sin and living unto God. And he would hereby guide us to make use of Christ and His death and resurrection by faith, as the powerful means of all holiness in heart and life ; and to increase in this manner of walking, until we attain unto perfection in Christ.

The *second* thing proposed was to lay before you. some

necessary instructions, that your steps may be guided aright to continue and go forward in this way of holiness, until you be made perfect in Christ. And we should pray earnestly, that God would give unto us the spirit of wisdom and revelation, that we may discern the way of holiness thereby, and walk aright in it, according to that gracious promise, "The wayfaring men, though fools, shall not err therein" (Isa. xxxv. 8).

1. Let us observe and consider diligently in our whole conversation, that though we are partakers of a new holy state by faith in Christ, yet our natural state doth remain in a measure with all its corrupt principles and properties. As long as we live in this present world our apprehension of Christ and His perfection in this life is only by faith; whereas by sense and reason we may apprehend much in ourselves contrary to Christ; and this faith is imperfect, so that true believers have cause to pray to God to help their unbelief (Mark ix. 24). Therefore though we receive a perfect Christ by faith, yet the measure and degree of enjoying Him is imperfect; and we hope still, so long as we are in this world, to enjoy Him in a higher degree of perfection than we have done. We are yet but weak in Christ (2 Cor. xiii. 4), children in comparison to the perfection we expect in another world (1 Cor. xiii. 10, 11); and we must grow still till we come to the perfect man (Eph. iv. 13); and some are weaker babes than others, and have received Christ in so small a measure that they may be accounted carnal rather than spiritual (1 Cor. iii. 1). And because all the blessings and perfections of our new state—as justification, the gift of the Spirit, and of the holy nature, and the adoption of children—are seated and treasured up in Christ, and joined with Him inseparably, we can receive them no further than we receive Christ Himself by faith, which we do in an imperfect measure and degree in this life.

They are said to be not in the flesh but in the Spirit, because their being in the Spirit is their best and lasting state, as denominations are usually taken from the better part, but yet the flesh is in them, and they find work enough to mortify the deeds of it (Rom. viii. 9, 13).

2. Despair of purging the flesh or natural man of its sinful lusts and inclinations, and of practising holiness by your willing and resolving to do the best that lieth in your own power, and trusting on the grace of God and Christ to help you in such resolutions and endeavours; rather resolve to *trust on Christ to work in you* to will and to do by His own power according to His own good pleasure. They that are convinced of their own sin and misery do commonly first think to tame the flesh, and to subdue and root out its lusts, and to make their corrupt nature to be better natured and inclined to holiness by their struggling and wrestling with it; and if they can but bring their hearts to a full purpose and resolution to do the best that lieth in them, they hope that by such a resolution they shall be able to achieve great enterprises in the conquests of their lusts and performance of the most difficult duties. It is the great work of some zealous divines in their preaching and writings to stir up people to this resolution, wherein they place the chiefest turning point from sin to godliness. And they think that this is not contrary to the life of faith, because *they trust on the grace of God through Christ to help them* in all such resolutions and endeavours. Thus they endeavour to reform their old state and to be made perfect in the flesh, instead of putting it off and walking according to the new state in Christ. They trust on low carnal things for holiness, and upon the acts of their own will, their purposes, resolutions, and endeavours, instead of Christ; and *they trust to Christ to help them* in this carnal way; whereas true faith would teach them that they are nothing, and that they do but labour in vain.

They may as well attempt to wash a Blackamoor white as to purge the flesh or natural man from its evil lusts, and make it pure and holy. It is desperately wicked, past all cure. They that would cure the flesh and make it holy by their own resolutions and endeavours, do act quite con-

trary to the design of Christ's death : for He died, not
that the flesh or old natural man might be made holy, but
that it might be crucified and destroyed out of us (Rom.
vi. 6), and that we might live to God, and not to ourselves, not by any natural power of our own resolutions or
endeavours, but by Christ living in us, and by His Spirit
bringing forth the fruits of righteousness in us (Gal. ii. 20,
and v. 24, 25). Therefore we must be content to leave
the natural man vile and wicked as we found it, until it
be utterly abolished by death. Our way to mortify sinful affections and lusts must be not by purging them
out of the flesh, but by putting off the flesh itself, and
*getting above into Christ by faith, and walking in that
new nature that is by Him.* Thus, "the way of life
is above to the wise, that he may depart from hell beneath" (Prov. xv. 24). Our willing, resolving, and endeavouring must be *to do the best,* not that lieth in ourselves, or in our own power, but *that Christ and the power
of His Spirit shall be pleased to work in us ;* for in us—
*i.e.,* in our flesh—there dwelleth no good thing (Rom. vii.
18.) We have great ground to trust in God and Christ for
help in such resolutions and endeavours after holiness, as
in things that are agreeable to the design of Christ in our
redemption, and to the way of acting and living by faith.
*It is not enough for us to trust on Christ to help us* to act
and endeavour so far only as creatures, for so the worst of
men are helped ; He is the Jehovah in whom they live,
move, and have their being (Acts xvii. 28). And it is
likely the Pharisee would trust on God to help him in
duty, as he would thank God for the performance of duty
(Luke xviii. 11). And this is all the faith that many
make use of in order to a holy practice. But we must
*trust on Christ to enable us above the strength of our own
natural power* by virtue of *the new nature which we have
in Christ,* and by His Spirit dwelling and working in us ;
or else our best endeavours will be altogether sinful and
mere hypocrisy, notwithstanding all the help for which
we trust upon Him. We must also take heed of depend-

ing for holiness upon any resolution to walk in Christ, or upon any written covenants, or upon any holiness that we have already received; for we must know that the virtue of these things continues no longer than we continue walking in Christ and Christ in us. They must be kept up *by the continual presence of Christ in us,* as light is maintained by the presence of the sun, and cannot subsist without it.

3. You must not seek to procure forgiveness of sins, the favour of God, a new holy nature, life, and happiness, by any works of the moral law; but rather *you must work as those that have all these things already,* according to your new state in Christ; as such who are only to receive them more and more *by faith,* as they are ready prepared and treasured up for you, and freely given to you, in your spiritual Head, the Lord Jesus Christ. If we walk as those that are yet wholly to seek for the procurement of such enjoyments as these, it is a manifest sign that, at present, we judge ourselves to be without them, and without Christ Himself; in whose fulness they are all contained; and therefore we walk according to our old natural state, as those that are yet in the flesh, and that would get salvation in it, and by our carnal works and observances, instead of living altogether on Christ by faith.

This practice is according to the tenor of the covenant of works, as I have before showed. And we have no ground to trust on Christ and His Spirit to work holiness in us this way; for we are dead to the legal covenant by the body of Christ (Rom. vii. 4); and, "if we be led by the Spirit, we are not under the law" (Gal. v. 18). When the Galatians were seduced, by false teachers, to seek the procurement of justification and life by circumcision and other works of the Mosaical law, the Apostle Paul rebuketh them for seeking to be made perfect in the flesh, directly contrary to their good beginning in the Spirit, for rendering Christ of none effect to them, and for falling from grace (Gal. iii. 3, and v. 4). And, when some of the Colossians sought perfection in the like manner, by observation of circumcision, holy meats, holy times, and other rudiments of the world, the same apostle blameth them for not holding the head Jesus Christ, and as though they were not dead and risen with Christ, but living merely in the world (Col. ii. 19, 20, and iii. 1). He clearly showeth, that those who seek any saving enjoyments in such a way, do walk according to their old natural state ; and that the true manner of *living by faith* in Christ is, to walk as those that have all fulness and perfection of spiritual blessings in Christ by faith, and need not seek for them any other way to procure them for themselves. In this sense it is a true saying, That believers should not act *for* life, but *from* life. They must act as those that are not procuring life by their works, but as those who have already received and derived life from Christ, and act from the power and virtue received from Him.

4. Think not that you can effectually incline your heart to the immediate practice of holiness, by any such practical principles as do only serve to bind, press, and urge you to the performance of holy duties, but rather let such principles stir you up to go *to Christ first by faith*, that you may be effectually inclined to the immediate practice of holiness in Him by gospel principles, that strengthen and enable you, as well as oblige you there-unto. There are some practical principles that do only bind, press, and urge us to holy duties, by showing the reasonableness, equity, and necessity of our obedience, with-out showing at all how we that are by nature dead in sin, under the wrath of God, may have any strength and ability for the performance of those duties ; as, for instance, the authority of God the lawgiver ; His all-seeing eye ; the un-speakable joy of heaven, and terrible damnation of hell ;— such principles as these do bind our consciences very strictly, and do work very strongly upon the prevalent affections of hope and fear, to press and urge our hearts to the per-formance of holy duties, if we believe them assuredly, and work them earnestly upon our hearts, by frequent, serious, lively meditation. And therefore some account

them the most forcible and effectual means to form any
virtue in the soul, and to bring it to immediate performance of any duty, though never so difficult, and that the
life of faith consisteth principally in our living to God in
holiness by a constant belief and meditation on them.

But this is not that manner of living to God whereof
the apostle speaketh, when he saith, "I live, yet not I,
but Christ liveth in me; and the life which I live in the
flesh, I live by the faith of the Son of God, who loved
me, and gave Himself for me" (Gal. ii. 20). If a man
make use of these obliging principles to stir him to go to
Christ for strength to act holily, he walketh like one that
hath received Christ as his only life by faith, otherwise
he walketh like other natural men. For the natural man
may be brought to act by these principles, partly by
natural light, and more fully by Scripture light, without
any true knowledge of the way of salvation by Christ,
and as if Christ had never come into the world. And he
may be strictly bound by them, and vehemently urged
and pressed to holy duties, and yet all this while is left
to his own natural strength, or rather weakness, being not
assured by any of these principles that God will give him
strength to help him in the performance of these duties;
and can do nothing aright until he get new life and
strength in Christ by a more precious saving faith. There
would be no need of a new life and strength by Christ, if
these principles were sufficient to bring us to a holy conversation. Therefore this manner of practice is no better
than walking after the flesh, according to our corrupt state,
and a seeking to be made perfect in the flesh.

And yet these obliging principles are very good and
excellent in this right gospel use of them; as the apostle
saith of the law, that it is good if it be used lawfully (1
Tim. i. 8). The humbled sinner knoweth well his obligations, but it is life and strength that he wanteth; and
he despaireth of walking according to such obligations until
he get this life and strength *by faith* in Christ. Therefore these obliging principles do move him to go, in the

first place, to Christ, that so he may be enabled to answer their end, by the strengthening and enlivening principles of God's grace in Christ.

Some there are that make use of gospel principles only to oblige and urge to duty, without affording any life and strength for the performance, as they that think Christ died and rose again to establish a new covenant of works for our salvation, and to give us a pattern of good works by His own obedience, rather than to purchase life, obedience, and good works for us. Such as these do not understand and receive the principles of the gospel rightly, but they pervert and abuse them, contrary to their true nature and design ; and thereby they render them as ineffectual for their sanctification as any other natural or legal principles.

5. Stir up and strengthen yourself to perform the duties of holiness, *by a firm persuasion of your enjoyment* of Jesus Christ, and all spiritual and everlasting benefits through Him.

Your way to a holy practice is, first to conquer and expel all unbelieving thoughts, by trusting confidently on Christ, and persuading yourselves by faith, that His righteousness, Spirit, glory, and all His spiritual benefits are yours ; and that He dwelleth in you, and you in Him. *In the might of this confidence,* you shall go forth to the performance of the law ; and you will be strong against sin and Satan, and able to do all things through Christ that strengthens you. *This confident persuasion* is of great necessity to the right framing and disposing our hearts to walk according to our new state in Christ. The *life of faith* principally consisteth in it. And herein it eminently appeareth, that faith is a hand, not only to receive Christ, but also to work by Him ; and that it cannot be effectual for our sanctification except it contain in it some assurance of our interest in Christ, as hath been showed. Thus we act as those that are above the sphere of nature, advanced to union and fellowship with Christ. The apostle maintained in His heart a persuasion that Christ had loved him,

and given Himself for Him; and hereby he was enabled
to live to God in holiness, through Christ living in him by
faith. He teacheth us also, that we must maintain the
like persuasion, if we would walk holily in Christ. We
must know that our old man is crucified with him; and
we must reckon ourselves dead indeed unto sin, and alive
unto God through Jesus Christ our Lord (Rom. vi. 6, 11).
This is the means whereby we may be filled with the
Spirit, strong in the Lord and in the power of His might;
which God would not require of us, if he had not appointed
the means (Eph. vi. 10).

Christ Himself walked in a constant persuasion of His
excellent state; He set the Lord always before Him, and
was persuaded that, because God was at His right hand,
He should not be moved (Ps. xvi. 8). How should it be
rationally expected, that a man should act according to
this new state, without assurance that he is in it? It is a
rule of common prudence in all worldly callings and conditions, that every one must know and well consider his
own state, lest he should act proudly above it, or sordidly
below it. And it is a hard thing to bring some to a right
estimate of their own worldly condition. If the same
rule were observed in spiritual things, doubtless the knowledge and persuasion of the glory and excellency of our
new state in Christ would more elevate the hearts of believers above all sordid slavery to their lusts, and enlarge
them to run cheerfully the ways of God's commandments.
*If Christians knew their own strength better, they would
enterprise greater things for the glory of God.* But this
knowledge is difficultly attained; it is only by faith and
spiritual illumination. The best know but in part; and
hence it is that the conversation of believers falleth so
much below their holy and heavenly calling.

6. Consider what endowments, privileges, or properties
of your new state are most meet and forcible to incline and
strengthen your heart to love God above all, and to re-
nounce all sin, and to give up yourself to universal obedience to His commands; and strive to walk in the persuasion

of them, that you may attain to the practice of these great duties. I may well join these together, because to love the Lord with all our heart, might, and soul, is the first and great commandment, which influenceth us to all obedience, with a hatred and detestation of all sin, as it is contrary and hateful to God. The same effectual means that produceth the one will also produce the other; and holiness chiefly consisteth in these.

For the same end, that your hearts may be rightly fitted and framed for the performance of these principal duties, the Holy Scriptures direct you to walk in the persuasion of other principal endowments of your new state, as, that you have fellowship with the Father, and with His Son Jesus Christ (1 John i. 3); and that you are the temple of the living God (2 Cor. vi. 16); that you live by the Spirit (Gal. v. 25); that you are called to holiness, and created in Christ Jesus unto good works; that God will sanctify you wholly, and make you perfect in holiness at the last (1 Thess. v. 23; Eph. ii. 10); that your old man is crucified with Christ; and that through Him " you are dead unto sin, and alive unto God; and being made free from sin, you are become the servants of righteousness, and have your fruit unto holiness, and the end everlasting life" (Rom. vi. 6, 22); "Ye are dead, and your life is hid with Christ in God. When Christ who is your life shall appear, then shall ye also appear with Him in glory" (Col. iii. 4). Such persuasions as these, when they are deeply rooted and constantly maintained in our hearts, do strongly arm and encourage us to practise universal obedience in opposition to every sinful lust; because we look upon it not only as our duty, but our great privilege, to do all things through Christ strengthening us; and God doth certainly work in us both to will and to do by these principles, because they properly belong to the gospel, or New Testament, which is the ministration of the Spirit, and the power of God unto salvation (2 Cor. iii. 6, 8; Rom. i. 16).

7. For the performance of other duties of the law, you are to consider not only these endowments, privileges, and properties of your new state, which are meet and forcible

**E**

to enable you to the love of God and universal obedience, but also those that have a peculiar force and aptitude suitable to the special nature of such particular duties ; and you must endeavour to assure yourselves of them by faith, that you may be encouraged and strengthened to perform the duties. I shall give you some instances of this manner of practice in several duties, whereby you may the better understand how to guide yourselves in the rest.

And as to the duties of the first table, if you would draw near to God in the duty of His *worship* with a true heart, you must do it in full assurance of faith concerning your enjoyment of Christ and His salvation. And would you perform the great duty of *trusting* on the Lord with all your heart, casting your care upon Him, and committing the disposal of yourself to Him in all your concerns ? Persuade yourself through Christ that God, according to His promise, will never fail you nor forsake you, that He taketh a fatherly care of you, that He will withhold no good thing from you, and will make all things to work for your good. And thus you will be strong and courageous in the practice of this duty.

That you may love your neighbour as yourself, and do to him in all things as you would he should do to you, without partiality and self-seeking; that you may give him his due honour, and abstain from injuring him, you must walk in a persuasion, not only that these things are just and equitable toward your fellow-creatures, and that you are strictly bound to the performance of them, but that they are the will of your heavenly Father, who hath begotten you according to His own image in righteousness and true holiness, and hath given you His Spirit that you may be like-minded to Him in all things; and that they are the mind of Christ, who dwelleth in you, and you in Him ; that God and Christ are kind, tender-hearted, long-suffering, full of goodness to men, whether good or bad, friends or enemies, poor or rich; and that Christ came into the world, not to destroy but to save, and that you are of the same spirit; that the injuries done to you by your neighbours can do you no harm, and you need not seek any good for yourselves by injuring them, because you have all desirable happiness in Christ; and all things, though intended by your enemies for your hurt, certainly work for your good through Christ. Such apprehensions as these, wrought in us by the Spirit of faith, do certainly beget in us a right frame of spirit, thoroughly furnished for every good work towards our neighbour.

Likewise your hearts will be purified to unfeigned love of the brethren in Christ, and you will walk toward them with all lowliness, meekness, long-suffering, forbearing one another in love, *if you maintain a steadfast belief and persuasion* of those manifold bonds of love whereby you are inseparably joined with them through Christ; as particularly that there is one body and one Spirit, one hope of your calling, one Lord, one faith, one baptism, one God and Father of all, who is above all, and through all, and in you all.

Finally, you will be able to abstain from all fleshly and worldly lusts, that war against the soul, and hinder all godliness, *by an assured persuasion,* not merely that gluttony, drunkenness, are filthy abominations, and that the pleasures, profits, and honours of the world are vain, empty things; but that you are crucified to the flesh and the world, and quickened, raised, and sit in heavenly places together with Christ; and that you have pleasures, profits, honours in Christ, to which the best things in the world are not worthy to be compared; and that you are members of Christ, the temple of His Spirit, citizens of heaven, children of the day, not of the night nor of darkness, *so that it is below your state and dignity* to practise deeds of darkness, and mind fleshly, worldly things.

8. If you endeavour to grow in grace, and in all holiness, trust assuredly *that God will enable* you, by this manner of walking, *to do everything that is necessary for His glory,* and your own everlasting salvation; and that He will graciously accept of that obedience through Christ which you are enabled to perform according to the measure of your faith, and pardon your failings, though you offend in many things, and fall short of many others, as to degrees of holiness and high acts of obedience. And therefore

attempt not the performance of duty in any other way, though you cannot yet attain to do so much in this way as you would. This is a necessary instruction to establish us in the life of faith, that the sense of our manifold failings and defects may not move us either to despair, or to return to the use of carnal principles and means for help against our corruptions, as accounting this way of living and acting by faith to be insufficient for our sanctification and salvation. We are to know, that though the law requireth of us the utmost perfection of holiness, yet the gospel maketh an allowance for our weakness, and Christ is so meek and lowly in heart that He accepteth of that which our weak faith can attain to by His grace, and doth not exact or expect any more of us for His glory and our salvation, until we grow stronger in grace. God showed His great indulgence to His people under the Old Testament, that Moses the lawgiver suffered them, because of the hardness of their hearts, to put away their wives, though from the beginning it was not so (Matt. xix. 8); and also in tolerating the customary practice of polygamy. Though Christ will not tolerate the continuance of such practices in His Church, since His Spirit is more plentifully poured forth under the gospel, yet He is as forward as ever to bear with the failings of His weak saints that desire to obey Him sincerely.

We are to beware of being too rigorous in exacting righteousness of ourselves and others, beyond the measure of faith and grace. Overdoing commonly proveth undoing. Children that venture on their feet beyond their strength have many a fall; and so have babes in Christ, when they venture unnecessarily upon such duties as are beyond the strength of their faith. We should be content, at present, to do the best that we can, according to the measure of the gift of Christ, though we know that others are enabled to do much better; and we are not to despise the day of small things, but to praise God, that He worketh in us anything that is well pleasing in His sight, hoping that He will sanctify us throughout, and bring us at last to perfection of holiness through Jesus Christ our Lord.

# CHAPTER XIII.

## THE MEANS OF HOLINESS TO BE USED IN FAITH.

---

### DIRECTION.

Endeavour diligently to make the *right use of all means* appointed in the Word of God, for the obtaining and practising Holiness, *only in this way of believing in Christ, and walking in Him according to your new state by faith.*

Two things are observable in this direction :—

*First*, Though all holiness be effectually attained by the life of faith in Christ, yet the use of any means appointed in the Word for attaining and promoting holiness, is not hereby made void, but rather established.

We do indeed assert and profess, that a true and lively faith in Christ is alone sufficient and effectual, through the grace of God, to receive Christ and all His fulness, so far as is necessary in this life, for our justification, sanctification, and eternal salvation; but yet we also assert and profess, that several means are appointed of God for the begetting, maintaining, and increasing this faith, and the acting and exercising it in order to the attainment of its end ; and that these means, which are mentioned in the sequel, are to be used diligently.

The *second* thing observable and principally designed in this direction is, the *right manner* of using all the means of holiness for the obtaining and practising it in no other way besides that of believing in Christ, and walking in Him according to our new state by faith; which hath been already demonstrated to be the only way whereby we may effectually attain to this great end. We must use them as helps to the life of faith in its beginning, continu-

ance, and growth; and as instruments subservient to faith,
the principal instrument, in all its acts and exercises,
whereby the soul receiveth Christ, and walketh in all
holiness by Him. We must beware lest we use them
rather in opposition than in subordination to the way of
sanctification and salvation by free grace in Christ through
faith; and lest, by our abuse of them, they be made rather
hindrances than helps to our faith. For God's ordinances are
like the cherubims of glory made with their faces looking
towards the mercy-seat. They are made to guide us to
Christ for salvation by faith alone. This right use of the
means of grace is a point wherein many are ignorant that
use them with great zeal and diligence ; and thereby they
do not only lose their labour, and the benefit of the means,
but also they wrest and pervert them to their own destruction.

That you may not stumble and fall by the same pernicious error, I shall show particularly how several of the
principal means of holiness appointed in the Word of God
are to be made use of in that right manner expressed in
the direction :—

We must endeavour diligently to *know the Word of God*
contained in the Holy Scriptures, and to improve it to this
end, that we may be made wise unto salvation through faith
which is in Christ Jesus (2 Tim. iii. 15). But here our
great work must be to get such a knowledge of the Word
as is necessary and sufficient to guide us in receiving
Christ, and walking in Him by faith.

The most effectual knowledge for your salvation is to
understand these two points—the desperate sinfulness and
misery of your own natural condition, and the alone suffi-
ciency of the grace of God in Christ for your salvation—
that you may be abased as to the flesh, and exalted in
Christ alone.

You also should learn the true difference between the
two covenants, the old and the new, or the law and the
gospel ; that the former shutteth us up under the guilt
and power of sin, and the wrath of God and His curse,
by its rigorous terms, " Do all the commandments and
live," and " Cursed are you, if you do them not, and fail

in the least point;" the latter (*i.e.*, the new covenant) openeth the gates of righteousness and life to all believers by its gracious terms, "Believe in the Lord Jesus Christ, and live—*i.e.*, all your sins shall be forgiven, and holiness and glory shall be given to you freely by His merit and Spirit." Furthermore, you should learn the gospel principles that you are to walk by for the attainment of holiness in Christ. And here I shall mind you particularly, that you would be a good proficient in Christian learning, if you were to get a good understanding of the 6th and 7th chapters of the Epistle of the Apostle Paul to the Romans, where the powerful principles of sanctification are purposely treated of and differenced from those weak and ineffectual principles which we are most naturally prone to walk by.

Another means to be used diligently for the promoting the life of faith is, *examination* of our state and ways according to the Word. But your great care in this work of self-examination must be to perform it in such a manner that it may not hinder and destroy the life of faith, as it doth in many, instead of promoting it. Therefore, beware lest you trust upon your self-examination, rather than upon Christ.

Misspend not your time, as many do, in poring upon your hearts, to find whether you be good enough to trust on Christ for your salvation, or to find whether you have any faith, before you dare be so bold as to act faith in Christ. But know, that though you cannot find that you have any faith or holiness, yet, if you will now believe on Him that justifieth the ungodly, it shall be accounted to you for righteousness (Rom. iv. 5).

*Meditation* on the Word of God is of very great use and advantage for the attainment and practice of holiness through faith in Christ. It is a duty whereby the soul doth feed and ruminate upon the Word as its spiritual food, and digesteth it, and turneth it into nourishment, whereby we are strengthened for every good work. Our souls are satisfied therewith, as with marrow and fatness, when we remember God upon our bed, and meditate on

Him in the night-watches (Ps. lxiii. 5, 6). The new
nature may well be called "the mind" (Rom. vii. 25),
because it liveth and acteth by minding and meditating on
spiritual things. Therefore it is a duty to be practised,
not only at some limited times, but all the day (Ps. cxix.
97); yea, day and night (Ps. i. 2); even in our ordinary
employments at home and abroad. An habitual knowledge
of the Word will not profit us without an active minding
it by frequent meditation.

But here our greatest skill and chiefest concernment
lie in practising this duty in such a manner as that it
may be subservient, and not at all opposite to the life of
faith.

Meditation is indeed very useful to press upon our conscience the strictness of our obligation to holy duties, and
to move us to go by faith to Christ for life and strength to
perform them. But that we may receive this life and
strength, whereby we are enabled for immediate performance, we must meditate believingly on Christ's saving
benefits as they are discovered in the gospel, which is the
only doctrine which is the power of God to our salvation,
and whereby the quickening Spirit is ministered to us, and
that is able to build us up, and give us an inheritance
among all them which are sanctified (Rom. i. 16; 2 Cor.
iii. 6; Acts xx. 32). You must take special care to act
faith in your meditation, mix the word of God's grace with
it, or else it will not profit you (Heb. iv. 2). And if you
set the loving-kindness of God frequently before your
eyes, by meditating on it believingly, you will be strengthened to walk in the truth (Ps. xxvi. 3).

The sacrament of *baptism* must needs be of great use to
promote the life of faith, if it be made use of according to
its nature and institution, because it is a seal of the righteousness of faith, as circumcision was formerly (Rom.
iv. 11).

The sacrament of *the Lord's Supper* is as a spiritual
feast to nourish our faith, and to strengthen us to walk in
all holiness, by Christ living and working in us, if it be
used according to the pattern which Christ gave us in its

first institution, recorded by three Evangelists (Matt. xxvi. 26–28; Mark xiv. 22–24; Luke xxii. 19, 20).

Furthermore, this sacrament doth not only *put us in mind* of the spiritual blessings wherewith we are blessed in Christ, and our enjoyment of them by faith, but also it is *a mean and instrument* whereby God doth *really* exhibit and give forth Christ and His salvation to true believers, and whereby He doth stir up and strengthen believers to receive and feed upon Christ by present actings of faith, while they partake of the outward elements. When Christ saith, " Eat, drink ; this is My body, this is My blood ;" no less can be meant than that Christ doth as truly give His body and blood to true believers in that ordinance, as the bread and cup ; and they do as truly receive it by faith.

Therefore the Apostle Paul asserteth that the bread in the Lord's Supper is the communion of the body of Christ, and the cup is the communion of His blood (1 Cor. x. 16) ; which showeth that Christ's body and blood are really communicated to us, and we do really partake of them, as well as of the bread and cup. The chief excellency and advantage of this ordinance is, that it is not only a figure and resemblance of our living upon a crucified Saviour, but also a precious instrument, whereby Christ, the bread and drink of life, is really conveyed to us, and received by us through faith.

One reason why many do little esteem, and seldom or never partake of this ordinance, and do find little benefit by it, is because they falsely imagine that God in it only holds forth naked signs and resemblances of Christ and His salvation, which they account to be held forth so plainly in Scripture that they need not the help of such a sign ; whereas, if they understood that God doth really give Christ Himself to their faith, by and with those signs and resemblances, they would prize it as the most delicious feast, and be desirous to partake of it on all opportunities (Acts ii. 42, and xx. 7).

*Prayer* is to be made use of as a means of living by faith in Christ according to the new man ; and it is the

making our requests with supplication and thanksgiving.
That it is to be used so, as an eminent means, appears,
because God requireth it (1 Thess. v. 17; Rom. xii. 12);
it is our priestly work (1 Pet. ii. 5, compared with Ps.
cxli. 2); and the property of saints (1 Cor. i. 2); and
God is a God hearing prayer (Ps. lxv. 2). God will be
prayed to by His people for the benefit that He is minded
to bestow upon them, when once He hath enabled them
to pray; though at first He is found of them that seek
Him not (Ezek. xxxvi. 37; Phil. i. 19, 20); that He may
prepare them for thanksgiving, and make benefits double
benefits to them (Ps. lxvi. 16, 18, 19, and l. 15; 2 Cor.
i. 10, 11). Though His will be not changed by this
means, yet it is accomplished ordinarily, and His purpose
is to accomplish it, this way. And therefore, trusting
assuredly should not make us neglect, but rather perform,
this duty (2 Sam. vii. 27). Christ, the mediator of the
new covenant, by which justification and sanctification are
promised, is also the mediator for acceptance of our prayers
(Heb. iv. 15, 16). The Spirit that sanctifieth us, begetteth
us in Christ, and showeth the things of Christ to us, is
a Spirit of prayer (Zech. xii. 10; Gal. iv. 6). He is as
fire inflaming the soul, and making it to mount upward in
prayer to God. Prayerless people are dead to God. If
they are children of Zion, yet they are but still-born, dead
children that cry not (Acts ix. 11); not written among
the living in Jerusalem; heathens in nature, though Christians in name (Jer. ix. 26). It is a duty so great, that it
is put for all the service of God as a fundamental duty,
which if it be done, the rest will be done well, and not
without it; and other ordinances of worship are helps to
it (Isa. lvi. 7). It is the great means whereby faith doth
exert itself to perform its whole work, and poureth itself
forth in all holy desires and affections (Ps. lxii. 8), and
so yields a sweet savour, as Mary's box of precious spike-
nard (Mark xiv. 3; John xii. 3); and so the same promises that are made to faith, are made also to prayer
(Rom. x. 11–13). It is our continual incense and sacrifice whereby we offer ourselves, our hearts, affections, and

lives, to God (Ps. cxli. 2). We act all grace in it, and must act it this way, or else we are not likely to act it any other way. And as we act grace, so we obtain grace by it, and all holiness (Ps. cxxxviii. 3; Luke xi. 13; Heb. iv. 16; Ps. lxxxi. 10). Our riches come in by it. Israel prevails while Moses holds up his hands (Exod. xvii. 11). By prayer Hannah is strengthened against her sorrows (1 Sam. i. 15, 18); peace is continued (Phil. iv. 6, 7); the disordered soul is set in order by it (as Hannah, 1 Sam. i. 18: Ps. xxxii. 1-5). Incense was still burnt, while the lamps were dressed (Exod. xxx. 7, 8). It is added to the spiritual armour, not as a particular piece of it, but as a means of putting on all, and making use of all aright that we may stand in the evil day (Eph. vi. 18). It is a means of transfiguring us into the likeness of Christ in holiness, and making our spiritual faces to shine, as Christ was transfigured bodily, whilst He prayed (Luke ix. 29); and Moses' face shone whilst he talked with God (Ex. xxxiv. 29).

Another means appointed of God, is *singing of psalms* —*i.e.*, songs of any sacred subject composed to a tune, hymns or songs of praise, and spiritual songs of any sublime spiritual matter, as Ps. xlv. and the Song of Solomon. God hath commanded it in the New Testament (Col. iii. 16; Eph. v. 19). You must use it for the same end as meditation and prayer, according to the nature of what is sung—*i.e.*, to quicken faith (2 Chron. xx. 21, 22; Acts xvi. 25, 26); and to stir up joy and delight in the Lord, glorying in Him (Ps. civ. 33, 34, cv. 3, cxlix. 1, 2, and xxxiii. 1-3). You are never right until you can be heartily merry in the Lord, and are able to act joy and mirth holily (Jas. v. 13; Eph. v. 19); and also to get more knowledge and instruction in heavenly mysteries, and in your duty, teaching and admonishing (Col. iii. 16).

*Fasting* is also an ordinance of God, to be used for the same purpose and end, and is commended to us under the New Testament, both by precept (Matt. ix. 15, and xvii. 21; 1 Cor. vii. 5); and example, as in Acts xiii. 2, 3, and xiv. 23). Use it as a help to extraordinary prayer and humiliation, that the mind may not be unsuited for these things, by eating, drinking, or bodily pleasures (Joel ii. 12 ; Isa. xxii. 12, 13 ; Zech. xii. 10–14). It is good only as a help to the soul, removing impediments. Some have not enough of spiritual-mindedness to give up themselves to fasting and prayer without great distraction; and such had better eat than go beyond their strength in a thing not absolutely necessary, which produceth only a slavish act, as in the case of virginity (1 Cor. vii. 7–9, 34–36).

Another great mean is, *fellowship and communion with the saints* (Acts ii. 42).

*First,* This mean must be used diligently. Whosoever God saveth should be added to some visible Church, and come into communion with other saints ; and if they have not opportunity for it their heart should be bent towards it. Sometimes the Church is in the wilderness, and hindered from visible communion and ordinances; but they that believe in Christ are always willing and desirous so to add and join themselves (Acts ii. 41, 44, 47). And they continued steadfastly in fellowship (1 John ii. 19).

*Second,* The means must be used rightly for the attaining of holiness only in Christ.

One rule is, Do not trust on church-membership, or on Churches, as if this or that relation in fellowship commended you to God of itself; whereas, a church-way is but a help to fellowship with Christ, and to walking in the duties of that fellowship.

Keep communion with a Church for the sake of communion with Christ (1 John i. 3 ; Zech. viii. 23). Therefore you must keep communion in Christ's pure ways only, and in them seek Christ by faith, that in the enjoyment of those advantages you may receive and act the godliness and holiness forementioned, and aim at spiritual flourishing and growth in grace. Choose, therefore, fellowship with the most spiritual Churches. Judge of Churches and men according to the rule of the new creature (2 Cor. v. 16, 17), and try them (Rev. ii. 2, and iii. 9), otherwise a Church may corrupt you.

# CHAPTER XIV.

## *THE EXCELLENCE OF THIS WAY OF HOLINESS.*

---

### DIRECTION.

That you may seek Holiness and Righteousness only by believing in Christ, and walking in Him by faith, according to
the former directions, take encouragement from *the great
advantages of this way, and the excellent properties of it.*

THIS direction may serve as an epilogue or conclusion, to
stir us up, by several weighty motives, unto a lively and
cheerful embracing those gospel rules before mentioned.
Many are kept from seeking godliness because they know
not the way to it; or the way that they think of seems
uncouth, unpleasant, disadvantageous, and full of dis-
couragement, like the way through the wilderness to
Canaan, which wearied the Israelites, and occasioned
their many murmurings (Num. xxi. 4).

But this is a way so good and excellent, that those that
have the true knowledge of it, and desire heartily to be
godly, cannot dislike it. I shall show the excellency of
it in several particulars. But you should first call to mind
what is the way I have taught—viz., union and fellowship
with Christ, and by faith in Christ as discovered in the
gospel; not by the law, or in a natural condition, or by
thinking to get it before we come to Christ, to procure
Christ by it, which is striving against the stream; but
that we must first apply Christ and His salvation to our-

selves for our comfort, and that by confident faith; and then walk by that faith according to the new man, in Christ and not as in a natural condition; and use all means of holiness rightly for this end.   Now, that this is an excellent, advantageous way, appears by the following desirable properties of it :—

*1st*, It hath this property, that it tends to the abasement of all flesh, and exaltation of God only, in His grace and power through Christ.  And so it is agreeable to God's design in all His works, and the end that He aimeth at (Eph. i. 6 ; Isa. ii. 17 ; Ezek. xxxvi. 21–23, 31, 32 ; Prov. xvi. 4), and a fit means for the attaining the end that we ought to aim at in the first place, which is the hallowing, sanctifying, and glorifying God's name in all things.  And this property of it is a great argument to prove that it is the way of God, and hath the character of His image stamped upon it.  We may say that it is like Him, and a way according to His heart, as Christ proveth His doctrine to be of God by this argument (John vii. 18). And Paul proveth the doctrine of justification and of sanctification, and salvation by grace through faith, to be of God, because it excludes all boastings of the creature (Rom. iii. 27, 28 ; 1 Cor. i. 29–31 ; Eph. ii. 8, 9).   This property appears evidently in the mystery of sanctification by Christ in us through faith.

It showeth that all our good works, and living to God, are not by our own power and strength at all, but by the power of Christ living in us by faith, and that God enableth us to act not merely according to our natural power, as He enableth carnal men and all other creatures, but above our own power, by Christ united to us and in us through the Spirit.  All men live, move, and have their being in Him; and by His universal support and maintenance of nature in its being and activity, they act (Heb. i. 3), so that the glory of their acting as creatures belongs to God.   But God acts more immediately in His people, who are one flesh and one spirit with Christ, and act not by their own power, but by the power of the Spirit of

Christ in them, as closely united to Him, and being the
living temples of His Spirit; so that Christ is the immediate principal agent of all their good works; and they
are Christ's works properly, who works all our works in
us and for us: and yet they are the saints' works by
fellowship with Christ, by whose light and power the
faculties of the saints do act (Gal. ii. 20; Eph. iii. 16, 17;
Col. i. 11), so that we are to ascribe all our works to God
in Christ, and thank Him for them as free gifts (1 Cor.
xv. 10; Phil. i. 11). God enableth us to act, not by ourselves, as He doth others, but by Himself. The wicked
are supported in acting only according to their own nature,
so they act wickedly. Thus all are said to live, move, and
have their being in God (Acts xvii. 28). But God enableth us to conquer sin, not by ourselves, but by Himself
(Hosea i. 7); and the glory of enabling us doth not only
belong to Him, which the Pharisee could not but ascribe
to Him (Luke xviii. 11), but also the glory of doing all in
us. And yet *we work as one with Christ*, even as He works
as one with the Father, by the Father working in Him.
We live as branches by the juice of the Vine, act as members by the animal spirits of the Head, and bring forth
fruit by marriage to Him as our Husband, and work in
the strength of Him as the living Bread that we feed on.
He is all in the new man (Col. iii. 11), and all the promises are made good in Him (2 Cor. i. 20).

2*d*, It hath this property, that it consisteth well with
other doctrines of the gospel, which contrary errors do not.

It confirms us in the doctrine of real union with Christ,
so plentifully held forth in Scripture; which doctrine some
account a vain notion, and cannot endure it, because they
think it worketh not holiness, but presumption; whereas
I have showed that it is absolutely necessary for the enjoyment of spiritual life and holiness, which is treasured
up in Christ; and *that* so inseparably, that we cannot
have it without a real union with Him (2 Cor. xiii. 5; 1
John v. 12; John vi. 53; and xv. 5; 1 Cor. i. 30; Col.
iii. 11). The members cannot live without union with the

head, nor the branches without union with the vine; nor can the stones be part of the living temple, except they be really joined mediately or immediately to the corner-stone.

3*d*, It hath this excellent property, that it is the never-failing, effectually-powerful, alone-sufficient, and sure way to attain to true holiness. They that have the truth in them find it, and the truly humble find it. People strive in vain when they seek it in any other way; therefore venture with the lepers, else you die (2 Kings vii.; Isa. lv. 2, 3, 7).

We cannot work holiness in ourselves (Rom. v. 6). So that an humbled person finds it in vain to seek holiness by the law or his own strength, for the law is weak through our flesh. Seeking a pure life without a pure nature, is building without a foundation. And there is no seeking a new nature from the law, for it bids us make brick without straw, and saith to the cripple, Walk, without giving any strength.

In this way only, we have a new and divine nature by the Spirit of Christ in us, effectually carrying us forth to holiness with life and love (Rom. viii. 5; Gal. v. 17; 2 Pet. i. 3, 4), and have new hearts according to the law; so that we serve God heartily, according to the new nature, and cannot but serve him (1 John iii. 9). So that here is a sure foundation for godliness, and love to God with all our heart, might, and soul; and sin is not only restrained, but mortified; and not only the outside made clean, but the inside, and the image of God renewed; and holy actings surely follow. We sin not according to the new nature; though we are not perfect in degree, because of the old nature.

4*th*, It is a most pleasant way to those that are in it (Prov. iii. 17), and that in several respects :—

1. It is a most *plain* way—easy to be found to one that seeth his own deadness under the law, and is so renewed in the spirit of his mind as to know and be persuaded of the truth of the gospel. The enlightened soul cannot think of another way when truly humbled (John vi. 68).

And when we are in Christ, we have His Spirit to be our guide in this way (1 John ii. 27 ; John xvi. 13).

2. It is *easy* to those that walk in it by the Spirit, though it be difficult to get into it, by reason of the opposition of the flesh or devil scaring us, or seducing us from it. Here you have *holiness as a free gift* received by faith, an act of the mind and soul. Whosoever will may come, take it, and drink freely ; and nothing is required but a willing mind (John vii. 37 ; Isa. lv. 1 ; Rev. xxii. 17). But the law is an intolerable burden (Matt. xxiii. 4 ; Acts xv. 10), if duty be laid on us by its terms. We are not left in this way to conquer lusts by our endeavours, which is a successless work ; but what is duty is given, and the law is turned into promises (Heb. viii. ; Ezek. xxxvi. 25, 27 ; Jer. xxxi. 33, and xxxii. 40). We have all now in Christ (Col. iii. 11, and ii. 9, 10, 15–17). This is a catholic medicine, instead of a thousand. How pleasant would this free gift—holiness—be to us, if we knew our own wants, inabilities, and sinfulness ! How ready are some to toil continually, and macerate their bodies in a melancholy legal way to get holiness, rather than perish for ever ! And, therefore, how ready should we be, when it is only, Take, and have ; Believe, and be sanctified and saved ! (2 Kings v. 13.) Christ's burden is light, by His Spirit's bearing it (Matt. xi. 30). No weariness, but renewing of strength (Isa. xl. 31).

3. It is a *way of peace* (Prov. iii. 17), free from fears and terrors of conscience, that those meet with unavoidably who seek salvation by works ; for the law worketh wrath (Rom. iv. 15). It is not the way of Mount Sinai, but of Jerusalem (Heb. xii. 18, 22). The doubts of salvation that people meet with, arise from putting some condition of works between Christ and themselves ; as hath appeared in this discourse. But our walking in this way is by faith, which rejects such fears and doubtings (John xiv. 1 ; Mark v. 36 ; Heb. x. 19, 22). It is free from fears of Satan or any evil (Rom. viii. 31–39) ; and free from slavish fears of perishing by our sins (1 John ii.

F

1, 2; Phil. iv. 6, 7); faith laying hold on infinite grace, mercy, and power to secure us; the Lord is the keeper and shade on the right hand (Ps. cxxi. 5). Free and powerful grace answers all objections.

4. It is a way that is *paved with love,* like Solomon's chariot (Song iii. 10). We are to set God's lovingkindness, and all the gifts of His love, still before our eyes (Ps. xxvi. 3); Christ's death, resurrection, intercession, before our eyes; which breed peace, joy, hope, love (Rom. xv. 13; Isa. xxxv. 10). You must believe for your justification, adoption, the gift of the Spirit, and a future inheritance, your death and resurrection with Christ. In believing for these things your whole way is adorned with flowers, and hath these fruits growing on each side; so that it is throught he garden of Eden, rather than the wilderness of Sinai (Acts ix. 31). It is the office of the Spirit or Guide to be our Comforter, and not a spirit of bondage (Rom. viii. 15). Peace and joy are great duties in this way (Phil. iv. 4–6).

5. Our very moving, acting, walking in this way, is *a pleasure and delight.* Every good work is done with pleasure; the very labour of the way is pleasant. Carnal men wish duties were not necessary, and they are burdensome to them; but they are pleasant to us, because we do not gain holiness by our own carnal wrestling with our lusts, and crossing them, out of carnal fear, with regret and grief, and setting conscience and the law against them to hinder their actings; but *we act naturally according to the new nature,* and perform our new spiritual desires by walking in the ways of God through Christ; and our lusts and pleasures in sin are not only restrained, but taken away in Christ; and pleasures in holiness freely given us and implanted in us (Rom. viii. 5; Gal. v. 17, 24; John iv. 34; Ps. xl. 8, and cxix. 14, 16, 20). We have a new taste and savour, love and liking, by the Spirit of Christ; and look on the law, not as a burden, but as our privilege in Christ.

5*th,* It is *a high exalted way,* above all other ways.

Unto this way the prophet Habakkuk is exalted, when, upon the failure of all-visible helps and supports, he resolves to rejoice in the Lord, and joy in the God of his salvation; and making God his strength by faith, is confident that his feet should be as hinds' feet, and that he should walk upon his high places (Hab. iii. 18, 19). These are the heavenly places in Christ Jesus that God hath set us in, being quickened and raised up together with Him (Eph. ii. 5, 6).

1. We live high here; for we live not after the flesh, but after the Spirit, and Christ lives in us with all His fulness (Rom. viii. 1, 2; Gal. ii. 20, and v. 25). We walk in fellowship with God dwelling in us and walking in us (2 Cor. vi. 16, 18). And therefore our works are of higher price and excellency than the works of others; because "they are wrought in God" (John iii. 21); and are the fruits of God's Spirit (Gal. v. 22; Phil. i. 11). And we may know that they are accepted and good by our gospel principles, which others have not (Rom. vii. 6).

2. We are enabled to the most difficult duties (Phil. iv. 12, 13), and nothing is too hard for us. See the great works done by faith (Heb. xi.; Mark ix. 23); works that carnal men think folly and madness to venture upon (they are so great), and honourable achievements, in doing and suffering for Christ.

3. We walk in an honourable state with God, and on honourable terms; not as guilty creatures to get our pardon by works—nor as bond-servants, to earn our meat and drink; but as sons and heirs, walking towards the full possession of that happiness to which we have a title; and so we have much boldness in God's presence (Gal. iv. 6, 7). We can approach nearer to God than others, and walk before him confidently without slavish fear; not as strangers, but as those who are of His own family (Eph. ii. 19, 20). And this prompts us to do greater things than others; walking as free men (Rom. vi. 17, 18; John viii. 35, 36). It is a kingly way; the law to us is a

royal law, a law of liberty, and our privilege; not a bond and yoke of compulsion.

4. It is the way only of those that are honourable and precious in the eyes of the Lord, even His elect and redeemed ones, whose special privilege it is to walk therein; no unclean beast goeth there (Isa. xxxv. 8, 9). No carnal man can walk in this way, but only those that are taught of God (John vi. 44–46). Nor would it have come into our hearts without Divine revelation (1 Cor. ii. 6–10).

5. The preparing this way cost Christ very dear. It is a costly way (Heb. x. 19, 20; 1 Pet. iii. 18).

6. It is a good old way, wherein thou mayest follow the footsteps of all the flock (Jer. vi. 16; Song i. 8).

7. It is the way to perfection. It leads to such holiness as shall in a while be absolutely perfect. It differs only in the degree and manner of manifestation from the holiness of heaven; *there* the saints live by the same Spirit, and the same God is all in all (1 Cor. xv. 28; John iv. 14); and have the image of the same spiritual man (1 Cor. xv. 49). *Here* we have but the first-fruits of the Spirit (Rom. viii. 23); and live by faith, and not by sight (2 Cor. v. 7); and are not full grown in Christ (Eph. iv. 13). Sanctification in Christ is glorification begun, as glorification is sanctification perfected.

THE END.

PRINTED BY BALLANTYNE, HANSON, AND CO.
EDINBURGH AND LONDON.

# JAMES NISBET & CO.'S
## LIST OF
# NEW AND RECENT PUBLICATIONS.

THE EMPIRE OF THE HITTITES. By WM. WRIGHT, B.A., D.D.
With Decipherment of Hittite Inscriptions by Professor SAYCE, LL.D.; a Hittite Map
by Col. Sir CHARLES WILSON, F.R.S., and Captain CONDER, R.E.; and a complete Set
of Hittite Inscriptions by W. H. RYLANDS, F.S.A. Royal 8vo, cloth, 17s. 6d.

ALIKE AND PERFECT. By the Rev. C. A. WILLIAMS. Crown
8vo, cloth, 3s. 6d.

A NEW TRANSLATION OF THE OLD TESTAMENT. Demy
8vo, cloth, 10s. 6d.

FROM THE BEGINNING TO THE GLORY; or, Scripture Lessons
for Bible Classes and Senior Classes in Sunday Schools. By Lady BEAUJOLOIS DENT.
Crown 8vo, cloth, 3s. 6d.

THE BOOK OF DANIEL. By the Rev. Professor MURPHY, D.D.
Crown 8vo, cloth, 3s.

SICK-ROOM MEDITATIONS; or, Alone with God. By the Rev.
J. CROSS, D.D., LL.D., author of "Evangel," &c. Crown 8vo, cloth, 5s.

INSPIRATION. A CLERICAL SYMPOSIUM on In what sense
and within what limits is the Bible the Word of God. By the Ven. ARCHDEACON
FARRAR, the Rev. PRINCIPAL CAIRNS, the Rev. PREBENDARY STANLEY LEATHES,
the Rev. PREBENDARY ROW, the Rev. Prof. J. RADFORD THOMSON, the Right Rev.
the BISHOP OF AMYCLA, and others. (Reprinted from the "Homiletic Magazine.")
Crown 8vo, cloth, 6s.

THE ATONEMENT: A CLERICAL SYMPOSIUM. By Various
Writers. Among the contributors are the Ven. Archdeacon FARRAR, D.D., Professor
ISRAEL ABRAHAMS, Rev. G. W. OLVER, Principal RAINY, D.D., The Bishop of
AMYCLA, and others. (Reprinted from the "Homiletic Magazine.") Crown 8vo,
cloth, 6s.

THE TEACHING OF THE APOSTLES: A Page of First Century
Christian Life, with Translation, Notes, and Dissertations. By CANON SPENCE, D.D.,
vicar of St. Pancras. Crown 8vo, 6s.

LIFE SONGS. With Illuminations and Illustrations in rich colours.
By the Marchioness of WATERFORD and the Countess of TANKERVILLE. Royal 4to,
£2 2s.

FOURSQUARE; or, The City of Our King. By M. M. Small
crown 8vo, cloth, 2s. 6d.

COMFORT. By Mrs. BESEMERES. 16mo, cloth, 1s.

VANISHED FACES. By the same. 16mo, cloth, 1s.

LAYS AND BALLADS OF HEROISM. By H. J. BARKER. Small
crown 8vo, paper covers, 1s.

**LIKE CHRIST.** A Sequel to "Abide in Christ." By the Rev. A. MURRAY. Small crown 8vo, cloth, 2s. 6d.

**THE GOSPEL AND THE CHILD.** By A. S. LAMB, Barrister-at-Law. Crown 8vo, cloth, 3s. 6d.

**LIFE IN HOSPITAL.** By Sister LUCY. 16mo, cloth, 1s.

**THE CHRISTIAN'S JEWELS.** Readings from the Fathers on Faith, Hope, and Charity. By the Rev. J. LEARY, D.C.L. 16mo, 1s. 6d.

**THE HIGHWAY OF HOLINESS:** An abridgment (in the Author's own words) of The Gospel Mystery of Sanctification. By the Rev. WALTER MARSHALL, with an introductory note by A. M. 16mo. cloth, 1s.

**SPIRIT FOOTPRINTS.** By Mrs. JOHN FOSTER. Square 16mo, cloth, 3s. 6d.

**MOMENTS ON THE MOUNT.** A Series of Devotional Meditations. By the Rev. GEORGE MATHESON, D.D., Author of "The Natural Elements of Revealed Theology," &c. Small crown 8vo, cloth, 3s. 6d.

**HIGH AIMS;** or, Romantic Stories of Christian Endeavour. By ELEANOR C. PRICE, Author of "A French Heiress," Crown 8vo, cloth, 5s.

**SAMUEL GOBAT,** Bishop of Jerusalem; His Life and Work. A Biographical Sketch, drawn chiefly from his own Journals. By his Son. Translated and Edited by Mrs. PEREIRA. Crown 8vo, cloth, with portrait and illustrations, 7s. 6d.

**THE GOSPEL IN GREAT BRITAIN.** By the Rev. S. McNAUGHTON. Crown 8vo, cloth, 3s. 6d.

**FURTHER RECOLLECTIONS OF AN INDIAN MISSIONARY.** By the Rev. J. S. LEUPOLT. Crown 8vo, cloth, 7s. 6d.

**CHOSEN, CHASTENED, CROWNED:** A Memoir of Mrs. SHEKLETON. With Portrait. Crown 8vo, cloth, 3s. 6d.

**A BOY'S WILL.** By ELLEN L. DAVIS. Crown 8vo, with illustrations, cloth, 2s.

**SUMMERLAND GRANGE.** By the LADY DUNBOYNE. Crown 8vo, with illustrations, cloth, 1s. 6d. ("Home and School Series.")

**AN UNWILLING WITNESS.** By Miss LYSTER. Crown 8vo, with illustrations, cloth, 3s. 6d.

**WHAT A MAN SOWETH.** By GRACE STEBBING. Crown 8vo, with illustrations, cloth, 3s. 6d.

**SUNDAY OCCUPATIONS.** By MARY BARCLAY. Small crown 8vo, cloth, 1s.

**SCRIPTURAL STUDIES.** By the Rev. CHARLES BRIDGES. Small crown 8vo, cloth, 2s. 6d.

**THE LAW OF JEHOVAH: BEING LECTURES ON THE** DECALOGUE. By the Rev. J. MATTHEW. Crown 8vo, cloth, 4s. 6d.

**OVER THE HOLY LAND.** By the Rev. J. A. WYLIE, LL.D. Author of "The History of Protestantism." Crown 8vo, cloth, 7s. 6d.

**CHARACTERISTICS OF CHRISTIANITY.** By the Rev. Professor STANLEY LEATHES, D.D. Crown 8vo, cloth, 6s.

**3**

OBSCURE CHARACTERS AND MINOR LIGHTS OF SCRIPTURE. By the Rev. FREDERICK HASTINGS. Crown 8vo, cloth, 5s.

THE PUBLIC MINISTRY AND PASTORAL METHODS OF OUR LORD. By the Rev. Professor BLAIKIE, D.D. Crown 8vo, cloth, 6s.

GLIMPSES THROUGH THE VEIL; or, Some Natural Analogies and Bible Types. By JAMES WARRING BARDSLEY, M.A., Author of "Illustrative Texts and Texts Illustrated." Crown 8vo, cloth, 5s.

MEMOIR OF THE REV. G. T. DODDS OF PARIS. By the Rev. HORATIUS BONAR, D.D. Crown 8vo, 6s.

LIFE OF MRS. STEWART SANDEMAN, OF BONSKEID AND SPRINGLAND. By Mrs. G. F. BARBOUR, Author of "The Way Home," &c. Crown 8vo, cloth, with several steel Engravings, 6s.

DRIFT LEAVES. By Mrs. HAYCRAFT (Miss MacRITCHIE). 16mo, cloth, 1s.

SONGS OF PEACE. By Mrs. HAYCRAFT, Author of "Waters of Quietness." 16mo, cloth, 1s.

ADDRESSES. By the Rev. FRANCIS PIGOU, D.D., Vicar of Halifax, Author of "Addresses on the Holy Communion." Small crown 8vo, cloth, 2s. 6d.

A MANUAL OF CONFIRMATION. By the Rev. FRANCIS PIGOU, D.D., Vicar of Halifax. Author of "Addresses on the Holy Communion," &c. Small crown 8vo, cloth, 3s. 6d

BUNYAN'S PILGRIM'S PROGRESS. (Red Line Edition.) Miniature Christian classics. Crown 32mo, cloth, 1s.; cloth gilt, 1s. 6d.

ABOUT OURSELVES. By Mrs. HENRY WOOD. Small crown 8vo, cloth, 1s. 6d.

STORY OF OUR ENGLISH BIBLE. By Mrs. BAYLY. Author of "Ragged Homes, and How to Win them." Crown 8vo, cloth, 3s. 6d.

STEPPING STONES TO HIGHER THINGS. By Captain SETON CHURCHILL. New Edition. Small crown 8vo, cloth, 2s. 6d.

CHURCH ORDINANCES. By Captain SETON CHURCHILL, Author of "Stepping Stones to Higher Things." Small Crown 8vo, cloth 2s. 6d.

THE WESTMINSTER ASSEMBLY: Its History and Standards. With some Account of English Puritanism up to the Meeting of the Assembly. Being the Baird Lecture for 1882. By the Rev. A. F. MITCHELL, D.D., Professor of Ecclesiastical History in St. Andrew's University. Crown 8vo, cloth, 10s. 6d.

ABRAHAM, THE FRIEND OF GOD: A Study from Old Testament History. By J. OSWALD DYKES, D.D. Post 8vo, cloth, 6s.

THE MANIFESTO OF THE KING. Comprising "The Beatitudes of the Kingdom," "The Laws of the Kingdom," and "The Relation of the Kingdom to the World." By the same. Crown 8vo, cloth, 6s.

A VOLUME OF FAMILY PRAYERS. By the same. Crown 8vo, cloth, 3s. 6d.

SERMONS. By the same. Crown 8vo, cloth, 5s.

EVENING STARS. By Mrs. EVERED POOLE. 32mo, cloth, 9d. (This volume is written on the plan intended to have been carried out by Miss F. R. Havergal, as described in the Preface to "Morning Stars.")

4

GOD'S ANSWERS: The narrative of Miss Annie Macpherson's Work at the Home of Industry, Spitalfields. By Miss LOWE, Author of "Punrooty." Crown 8vo, illustrated, cloth, 3s. 6d.

THE LORD'S PURSEBEARERS. By HESBA STRETTON. Crown 8vo, cloth, 1s. 6d.

PALESTINE EXPLORED. With a View to its Present Natural Features, and to the Prevailing Manners, Customs, Rites, and Colloquial Expressions of its People, which throw Light on the Figurative Language of the Bible. By the Rev. JAMES NEIL, M.A., Author of "Palestine Re-peopled," "Rays from the Realms of Nature," &c. Crown 8vo, cloth, illustrated, 6s.

THE NATURAL ELEMENTS OF REVEALED THEOLOGY: Being the Baird Lecture for 1881. By the Rev. GEORGE MATHESON, D.D., of Innellan. Crown 8vo, cloth, 6s.

SOLDIERS AND SERVANTS OF CHRIST; or, Chapters on Church History. With Preface by the Rev. F. V. MATHER, M.A., Vicar of St. Paul's, Clifton, and Canon of Bristol. Second edition. Crown 8vo, cloth, 5s.

SEEKING THE LOST. Incidents and Sketches of Christian Work in London. By the Rev. C. J. WHITMORE, Author of "The Bible in the Workshop." Crown 8vo, cloth, 3s. 6d.

BUNYAN'S PILGRIM'S PROGRESS. With 40 Illustrations, designed by Sir JOHN GILBERT, and engraved by W. H. WHYMPER. Printed on toned paper, and handsomely bound in cloth, 3s. 6d.; in leatherette, gilt edges, 5s.

ILLUSTRATIVE TEXTS AND TEXTS ILLUSTRATED. By the Rev. J. W. BARDSLEY, M.A. New and enlarged edition. Crown 8vo, cloth, 5s.

THE CULTURE OF PLEASURE; or, The Enjoyment of Life in its Social and Religious Aspects. By the Author of "The Mirage of Life." Fifth edition. Crown 8vo, cloth, 3s. 6d.

## Works by the Rev. CHARLES D. BELL, D.D.

SONGS IN MANY KEYS. Small crown 8vo, cloth, 5s.

VOICES FROM THE LAKES, and other Poems. Crown 8vo, cloth, 5s.

THE SAINTLY CALLING. Crown 8vo, cloth, 3s. 6d

HILLS THAT BRING PEACE. Crown 8vo, cloth, 5s.

NIGHT SCENES OF THE BIBLE, and their Teachings. First and Second Series. Crown 8vo, cloth, each 5s.

ADDITIONAL APPENDIX TO PSALMS AND HYMNS FOR PUBLIC AND SOCIAL WORSHIP. 16mo, cloth limp, 9d.; boards, 1s.

SONGS IN THE TWILIGHT. Small crown 8vo, cloth, 3s. 6d.

LIVING TRUTHS FOR HEAD AND HEART. Crown 8vo, cloth, 3s. 6d.

HYMNS FOR THE CHURCH AND CHAMBER. Crown 8vo, cloth, 3s. 6d.

## Works by the Rev. ERNEST BOYS, M.A.

CONSECRATED RECREATION. 16mo, cloth, 1s.
MY LORD'S MONEY. 16mo, cloth, 1s.
REST UNTO YOUR SOULS. 16mo, cloth, 1s.
THE SURE FOUNDATION. 16mo, cloth, 1s.
LIFE OF CONSECRATION. 16mo, cloth, 1s.
FILLED WITH THE SPIRIT; or, Scriptural Studies about the Holy Ghost. 16mo, cloth, 1s.

## Works by the Rev. JAMES WELLS, M.A.

BIBLE ECHOES. Addresses to the Young. Small crown 8vo, cloth, 3s. 6d.
PARABLES OF JESUS. Crown 8vo, illustrated, cloth, 5s.
BIBLE CHILDREN. Studies for the Young. Small crown 8vo, illustrated, cloth, 3s. 6d.
BIBLE IMAGES. Small crown 8vo, illustrated, cloth, 3s. 6d.

## Works by Mrs. SIMPSON.

GATES AND DOORS. Square 16mo, cloth, 1s.
STEPS THROUGH THE STREAM; or, Daily Readings for a Month. With an Introduction by Mrs. BARBOUR, Author of "The Way Home," &c. 16mo, cloth, 1s.
BEAUTIFUL UPON THE MOUNTAINS. 16mo, cloth, 1s.
WELLS OF WATER. Square 16mo, cloth, 1s.
A PITCHER BROKEN AT THE FOUNTAIN. Royal 32mo, 3d.

## Works by LADY HOPE OF CARRIDEN.

OUR COFFEE ROOM. With Preface by Lieutenant-General Sir ARTHUR COTTON, R.E., K.C.S.I. Crown 8vo, cloth, 3s. 6d.
MORE ABOUT "OUR COFFEE-ROOM." Crown 8vo, cloth, 3s. 6d.
SUNRISE GLEAMS. A Series of Daily Readings for a Month. 16mo, cloth, 1s.
SUNSET RAYS. A Companion volume to "Sunrise Gleams." 16mo, cloth, 1s.
TOUCHES OF REAL LIFE. Crown 8vo, cloth, 5s.
A MAIDEN'S WORK. Crown 8vo, cloth, 5s.
SUNNY FOOTSTEPS; or, When I was a Child. Fcap 4to, cloth, 3s. 6d.
LINES OF LIGHT ON A DARK BACKGROUND. Small crown 8vo, cloth, 3s. 6d.
INVITATIONS. 16mo, cloth, 1s. 6d.; in a packet, 16mo, 1s.; or separately, 2d. each.

# NISBET'S MINIATURE CHRISTIAN CLASSICS.

Uniformly bound in cloth, 1s. each; and cloth gilt, gilt edges, 1s. 6d. Red Line Editions.

1. BOGATZKY'S GOLDEN TREASURY.
2. KEBLE'S CHRISTIAN YEAR.
3. THE IMITATION OF CHRIST (Thomas à Kempis).
4. THE POEMS OF GEORGE HERBERT.
5. BUNYAN'S PILGRIM'S PROGRESS.

## Works by the Rev. F. WHITFIELD, M.A.

SHADOWS OF THE GREAT SACRIFICE; or, The Altar, the Bekah, and the Shoe. 16mo, cloth, 1s.

THE SAVIOUR PROPHET. Lessons from the Life of Elisha. Crown 8vo, cloth, 3s. 6d.

VOICES FROM THE VALLEY TESTIFYING OF JESUS. Small crown 8vo, cloth, 3s. 6d.

HOLY FOOTPRINTS. 16mo, cloth, 1s. 6d.

FROM CANA TO BETHANY; or, Gleanings from our Lord's Life on Earth. 16mo, cloth, 1s. 6d.

TRUTH IN CHRIST. Small crown 8vo, cloth, 3s. 6d.

EARTHLY SHADOWS OF THE HEAVENLY KINGDOM. Small crown 8vo, cloth, 3s. 6d.

CHRIST IN THE WORD. Small crown 8vo, cloth, 3s. 6d.

THE SAVIOUR'S CALL. Small crown 8vo, cloth, 1s. 6d.

THE CHANGED ONES: Reflections on the Second Chapter of the Song of Solomon. 16mo, cloth, 1s.

THE TABERNACLE, PRIESTHOOD, & OFFERINGS OF ISRAEL. With 22 illustrations. Crown 8vo, cloth, 5s. New Edition.

WHAT THE SPIRIT SAITH. 16mo, cloth, 1s. 6d: *New edition.*

## Works by the Rev. G. S. BOWES, B.A.

SCRIPTURE ITSELF THE ILLUSTRATOR: A Manual of Illustrations Gathered from Scriptural Figures, Phrases, Types, Derivations, Chronology, Texts, &c. Small crown 8vo, cloth, 3s. 6d.

INFORMATION AND ILLUSTRATIONS FOR PREACHERS AND TEACHERS. Crown 8vo, cloth, 5s.

ILLUSTRATIVE GATHERINGS FOR PREACHERS AND TEACHERS. First and Second Series. Small crown 8vo, cloth, each 3s. 6d.

IN PROSPECT OF SUNDAY. Crown 8vo, cloth, 5s.

## Works by the Rev. JAMES HAMILTON, D.D.

A UNIFORM EDITION OF THE WORKS OF THE LATE JAMES HAMILTON, D.D., F.L.S. Complete in Six Volumes. Post 8vo, cloth, each 7s. 6d.

LIFE IN EARNEST. Six Lectures on Christian Activity and Ardour. 16mo, cloth, 1s. 6d.

THE MOUNT OF OLIVES, and other Lectures on Prayer. 16mo, cloth, 1s. 6d.

A MORNING BESIDE THE LAKE OF GALILEE. 16mo, cloth, 1s. 6d.

THE MOUNT OF OLIVES, and a Morning beside the Lake of Galilee. 16mo, cloth, 2s. 6d.

MOSES THE MAN OF GOD: A Series of Lectures. Small crown 8vo, cloth, 5s.

THE PEARL OF PARABLES. Notes on the Parable of the Prodigal Son. 16mo, cloth, 1s. 6d.

THE LIGHT TO THE PATH; or, What the Bible has been to Others, and What it can Do for Ourselves. 16mo, cloth, 1s. 6d.

LESSONS FROM THE GREAT BIOGRAPHY. Crown 8vo, cloth, 5s.

THE ROYAL PREACHER; being Lectures on Ecclesiastes. Crown 8vo, cloth, 3s. 6d.

EMBLEMS FROM EDEN. 16mo, cloth, 1s. 6d.

THE HAPPY HOME. Illustrations. 16mo, cloth, 1s. 6d.

CHRISTIAN CLASSICS (OUR): Readings from the Best Divines; with Notices Biographical and Critical. In Four Vols. Crown 8vo, cloth, 16s.

THE LIFE OF THE LATE JAMES HAMILTON, D.D., F.L.S. By the Rev. WILLIAM ARNOT, Edinburgh. With Portrait. Post 8vo, cloth, 7s. 6d.

## Works by the Rev. J. JACKSON WRAY.

THE MAN WITH THE KNAPSACK; or, The Miller of Burnham Lee. Small crown 8vo, cloth, illustrated, 1s.

JOHN WYCLIF. A Quincentenary Tribute. Small crown 8vo, cloth, 2s. 6d.

HONEST JOHN STALLIBRASS. Crown 8vo, cloth, plain, illustrated, 3s. 6d.; cloth, gilt, 5s.

THE CHRONICLES OF CAPSTAN CABIN. Crown 8vo, cloth, 3s. 6d.

MATTHEW MELLOWDEW. Crown 8vo, cloth, 5s.

NESTLETON MAGNA. Crown 8vo, cloth, 3s. 6d.; gilt edges, 5s.

PETER PENGELLY. Crown 8vo, cloth, 2s.

PAUL MEGGITT'S DELUSION. Crown 8vo, cloth, 3s. 6d.

A MAN, EVERY INCH OF HIM. Crown 8vo, cloth, 3s. 6d.

A NOBLE VINE. Crown 8vo, cloth, 3s. 6d.

LIGHT FROM THE OLD LAMP. Crown 8vo, cloth, 3s. 6d.

GARTON ROWLEY; or, Leaves from the Log of a Master Mariner. Crown 8vo, cloth, with illustrations, 3s. 6d.

8

## Works by MRS. MARSHALL.

SILVER CHIMES; or, Olive. A Story for Children. Crown 8vo, cloth, with illustrations, 5s.

GRANDMOTHER'S PICTURES. Crown 8vo, cloth, with illus., 2s.

HEATHERCLIFFE. Small crown 8vo, cloth, with illustrations, 1s.

STORIES OF THE CATHEDRAL CITIES OF ENGLAND. Crown 8vo, cloth. with illustrations, 5s.

POPPIES AND PANSIES. Crown 8vo, cloth, illustrated, 5s.

SIR VALENTINE'S VICTORY. Crown 8vo, cloth, illustrated, 3s. 6d.

REX AND REGINA. Crown 8vo, cloth, with illustrations, 5s.

DEWDROPS AND DIAMONDS. Crown 8vo, cloth, illustrated, 5s.

HEATHER AND HAREBELL. Crown 8vo, cloth, 5s.

RUBY AND PEARL; or, The Children at Castle Aylmer. A Story for Little Girls. Crown 8vo, cloth, 3s. 6d.

STELLAFONT ABBEY; or, Nothing New. Small crown 8vo, cloth, 2s. 6d.

MARJORY; or, The Gift of Peace. 16mo, cloth, illustrated, 1s. 6d.

THREE LITTLE BROTHERS. 16mo, cloth, illustrated, 1s. 6d.

THREE LITTLE SISTERS. 16mo, cloth, illustrated, 1s. 6d.

GRACE BUXTON; or, The Light of Home. 16mo, cloth, illus., 1s. 6d.

FRAMILODE HALL; or, Before Honour is Humility. 16mo, cloth, illustrated, 1s.

A CHIP OF THE OLD BLOCK. Being the Story of Lionel King of Kingsholme Court. 16mo, cloth, illustrated, 1s.

VIOLET IN THE SHADE. 16mo, cloth, illustrated, 1s.

LIGHT ON THE LILY; or, A Flower's Message. 16mo, cloth, illus., 1s.

A ROSE WITHOUT A THORN. 16mo, cloth, illustrated, 1s.

BETWEEN THE CLIFFS; or, Hal Forrester's Anchor. 16mo, cloth, illustrated, 1s.

TO-DAY AND YESTERDAY. A Story of Summer and Winter Holidays. 16mo, cloth, illustrated, 1s.

PRIMROSE; or, The Bells of Old Effingham. 16mo, cloth, illus., 1s.

THE LITTLE PEATCUTTERS; or, The Song of Love. 16mo, cloth, illustrated, 1s.

DAISY BRIGHT. 16mo, cloth, illustrated, 1s.

## Works by ANNA WARNER.

SHOES OF PEACE. 16mo, cloth, 1s.

THE BLUE FLAG AND THE CLOTH OF GOLD. Crown 8vo, cloth, illustrated, 2s. 6d.

TIRED CHRISTIANS. 16mo, cloth, 1s.

THE MELODY OF THE TWENTY-THIRD PSALM. Royal 32mo, cloth, 3d.

WAYFARING HYMNS, Original and Selected. Royal 32mo, cloth, 6d.

MOTHER'S QUEER THINGS. Crown 8vo, cloth, with illustrations, 2s. 6d.

THE LIGHT OF THE MORNING. 32mo, cloth, 10d.

THE OTHER SHORE. Royal 32mo, cloth, 1s.

THE FOURTH WATCH. Royal 32mo, cloth, 10d.

WHAT AILETH THEE? Crown 8vo, cloth, 3s. 6d.

## Works by AGNES GIBERNE.

BERYL AND PEARL. Crown 8vo, cloth, with illustrations, 5s.

OLD UMBRELLAS ; or, Clarrie and Her Mother. Crown 8vo, cloth
with illustrations, 2s.

DECIMA'S PROMISE. Crown 8vo, cloth, illustrated, 3s. 6d.

DAILY EVENING REST. 16mo, cloth, 2s. 6d.

KATHLEEN. Crown 8vo, cloth, with illustrations, 5s.

## Works by DARLEY DALE.

SEVEN SONS ; or, The Story of Malcolm and his Brothers. Crown
8vo, with illustrations, cloth, 5s.

CISSY'S TROUBLES. Crown 8vo, cloth, illustrated, 3s. 6d.

SPOILT GUY. By the same. Crown 8vo, cloth, illustrated, 2s. 6d.

## Works by ANNA SHIPTON.

RIVERS AMONG THE ROCKS ; or, Walking with God. Small
crown 8vo, cloth, 1s. ; paper covers, 8d.

GOD WITH US. Crown 8vo, cloth, 3s. 6d.

THE UPPER SPRINGS AND THE NETHER SPRINGS ; or,
Life Hid with Christ in God. Small crown 8vo, cloth, 2s. 6d.

THE BELIEVER'S PORTION. 32mo, sewed, 3d.

## Works by the Rev. J. R. MACDUFF, D.D.

KNOCKING. The Words of Jesus at the Door of the Heart. A
Sacred Monody. Square 16mo, cloth, 1s. 6d.

THE STORY OF A SHELL. With numerous illustrations. Small
quarto, cloth, 6s.

EARLY GRAVES : A Book for the Bereaved. Crown 8vo, cloth, 5s.

VOICES OF THE GOOD SHEPHERD AND SHADOWS OF THE
GREAT ROCK. 16mo, cloth, 1s. 6d.

HOSANNAS OF THE CHILDREN. Crown 8vo, cloth, 5s.

IN CHRISTO ; or, The Monogram of St. Paul. Crown 8vo, cloth, 5s.

PALMS OF ELIM ; or, Rest and Refreshment in the Valley. Crown
8vo, cloth, 5s.

EVENTIDE AT BETHEL ; or, The Night Dream of the Desert. An
Old Testament Chapter in Providence and Grace. Crown 8vo, cloth, 3s. 6d.

NOONTIDE AT SYCHAR ; or, The Story of Jacob's Well. A New
Testament Chapter in Providence and Grace. With Frontispiece and Vignette. Small
crown 8vo, cloth, 3s. 6d.

BRIGHTER THAN THE SUN ; or, Christ the Light of the World.
A Life of our Lord for the Young. With sixteen Full-page Illustrations by A. Rowan.
Small 4to, cloth, 7s. 6d. Cheap edition. Small 4to, 3s. 6d. Paper covers, 1s.

THE FOOTSTEPS OF ST. PETER. Being the Life and Times of
the Apostle. Illustrations. Crown 8vo, cloth, 5s.

Works by the Rev. J. R. MACDUFF—continued.

THE GATES OF PRAISE, and other Original Hymns, Poems, and Fragments of Verse. 16mo, cloth, 1s. 6d.

CLEFTS OF THE ROCK; or, The Believer's Grounds of Confidence in Christ. Crown 8vo, cloth, 5s.

THE HEALING WATERS OF ISRAEL; or, The Story of Naaman the Syrian. An Old Testament Chapter in Providence and Grace. Crown 8vo, cloth, 4s. 6d.

COMFORT YE, COMFORT YE. Being God's Words of Comfort Addressed to His Church in the last Twenty-seven Chapters of Isaiah. With Frontispiece. Crown 8vo, cloth, 5s.

ST. PAUL IN ROME; or, The Teachings, Fellowships, and Dying Testimony of the Great Apostle in the City of the Cæsars. Crown 8vo, cloth, 4s. 6d.

MEMORIES OF PATMOS; or, Some of the Great Words and Visions of the Apocalypse. With Frontispiece. Cheap Edition. Crown 8vo, cloth, 3s. 6d.

MEMORIES OF GENNESARET. With Frontispiece. Post 8vo, cloth, 6s. 6d.

MEMORIES OF BETHANY. With Frontispiece. Crown 8vo, cloth, 3s. 6d.

FOOTSTEPS OF ST. PAUL. Being a Life of the Apostle designed for Youth. Crown 8vo, cloth, with illustrations, 5s.

THE MORNING AND NIGHT WATCHES. In one vol. 16mo and royal 32mo, cloth, 1s. 6d.; separately sewed, 8d.; cloth, 1s.

THE MIND AND WORDS OF JESUS. In one vol. 16mo and royal 32mo, cloth, 1s. 6d.; separately, sewed, 8d.; cloth, 1s.

THE THOUGHTS OF GOD. 16mo, cloth, 1s. 6d.; Cheap Edition, 32mo, cloth, 1s.

THE THOUGHTS OF GOD AND THE WORDS OF JESUS. 16mo, cloth, 1s. 6d.

FAMILY PRAYERS. Small crown 8vo, cloth, 3s. 6d.

THE GRAPES OF ESHCOL; or, Gleanings from the Land of Promise. Crown 8vo, cloth, 3s. 6d.

## Works by the Rev. GEORGE EVERARD, M.A.

UP HIGH. Friendly Words to those within and to those without the Fold of Christ. 16mo, cloth, 1s. 6d.

EVERY EYE. Small crown 8vo, cloth, 2s. 6d.

"YOUR INNINGS." A Book for Boys, with a recommendatory letter from the Archbishop of York. Small crown 8vo, cloth, 1s. 6d.

HIS STEPS. Small crown 8vo, cloth, 1s. 6d.

BRIGHT AND FAIR. A Book for Young Ladies. 16mo, cloth, 1s.

STRONG AND FREE. A Book for Young Men. With a recommendatory letter by the Right Honourable the Earl of Shaftesbury. 16mo, limp cloth, 1s.; boards, 1s. 6d.

Works by the Rev. G. EVERARD—continued.

FOLLOW THE LEADER. 16mo, 1s. 6d.

IN SECRET. A Manual of Private Prayer. 16mo, cloth, 1s.

THE RIVER OF LIFE. 16mo, cloth, 1s.

DAY BY DAY; or, Counsels to Christians on the Details of Every-day Life. Small crown 8vo, cloth, 3s. Also 16mo, cloth, 1s. 6d.

STEPS ACROSS; or, Guidance and Help to the Anxious and Doubt-ful. A Companion Volume to "Day by Day." Small crown 8vo, cloth, 3s.

BEFORE HIS FOOTSTOOL. Family Prayers for One Month. Small crown 8vo, cloth, 3s.

HOME SUNDAYS; or, Help and Consolation from the Sanctuary. Small crown 8vo, cloth, 3s.

NOT YOUR OWN; or, Counsels to Young Christians. 16mo, cloth, 1s.

SAFE AND HAPPY. Words of Help and Encouragement to Young Women. With Prayers for Daily Use. 16mo, cloth, 1s.

EDIE'S LETTER; or, Talks with the Little Folks. Small 4to, cloth, 2s. 6d.

MY SPECTACLES: and What I Saw With Them. Uniform with "Not Your Own." 16mo, cloth, 1s.

LITTLE FOXES, and How to Catch Them. 18mo, cloth, 1s.

BENEATH THE CROSS: Counsels, Meditations, and Prayers for Communicants. 16mo, cloth, 1s.

THE WRONG TRAIN; or, Common Mistakes in Religion. Small crown 8vo. cloth. 1s. 6d.

THE HOLY TABLE. A Guide to the Lord's Supper. 64 pp., tinted cover, 4d.; sewed, 6d.; cloth, 6d.

NONE BUT JESUS; or, Christ is All from First to Last. 32mo, sewed, 4d.; cloth limp, 6d.

WELCOME HOME; or, Plain Teachings from the Prodigal Son. 32mo, sewed, 6d.; cloth, 8d.

THE HOME OF BETHANY; or, Christ revealed as the Teacher and Comforter of His People. 32mo, sewed, 4d.; cloth, 6d.

---

# LIST OF WORKS
## BY THE LATE
# FRANCES RIDLEY HAVERGAL.

THE COMPLETE POETICAL WORKS OF FRANCES RIDLEY HAVERGAL, including some Pieces never before published. 2 vols., crown 8vo, cloth, 12s.

IVY LEAVES: Being Thoughts for a Month, from Miss HAVERGAL'S Poems, with elegant coloured borders. 16mo, cloth, 1s.

LIFE ECHOES. By the late FRANCES RIDLEY HAVERGAL. With Twelve Coloured Illustrations by the Baroness HELGA VON CRAMM. Small 4to, cloth gilt, 12s.

Works by the late F. R. HAVERGAL—continued.

**SWISS LETTERS AND ALPINE POEMS.** With twelve illustrations of Alpine Scenery and Flowers by the Baroness HELGA VON CRAMM. Small 4to, cloth, extra gilt, 12s.

**LIFE CHORDS**; the Earlier and Later Poems of the late FRANCES RIDLEY HAVERGAL. With 12 Chromo-Lithographs of Alpine Scenery, &c., from designs by the Baroness HELGA VON CRAMM, in one of which is introduced a Portrait of the Author in the ninth year of her age. Small 4to, cloth gilt, 12s.

**LIFE MOSAIC:** "The Ministry of Song" and "Under the Surface," in One Vol. With 12 Coloured Illustrations of Alpine Flowers and Swiss Mountain and Lake Scenery, from drawings by the Baroness HELGA VON CRAMM. Beautifully printed by Kaufmann, of Lahr-Baden. Small 4to, with Illustrated Initials, Head-pieces, &c., cloth, gilt extra, small 4to, 12s.

**MORNING STARS;** or, Names of Christ for His Little Ones. Royal 32mo, cloth, 9d.

**MORNING BELLS;** being Waking Thoughts for the Little Ones. Royal 32mo, sewed, 6d.; cloth, 9d.

**LITTLE PILLOWS:** being Good Night Thoughts for the Little Ones. Royal 32mo, sewed, 6d.; cloth, 9d.

**BRUEY, A LITTLE WORKER FOR CHRIST.** Small crown 8vo. cloth, 3s. 6d.; cheap edition, limp cloth, 1s. 6d.; sewed, 1s.

**THE FOUR HAPPY DAYS.** A Story for Children. Seventh edition. 16mo, cloth, 1s.

**SONGS OF PEACE AND JOY.** Selected from "The Ministry of Song" and "Under the Surface." With Music by CHARLES H. PURDAY. Fcap 4to, cloth, gilt edges, 3s.; or in paper covers, 1s. 6d.

**BEN BRIGHTBOOTS,** and other True Stories. Crown 8vo, cloth, 1s. 6d.

---

## ROYAL GRACE AND LOYAL GIFTS.

Comprising the following Seven Books in a neat cloth case, price 10s. The Books may be had separately, 16mo, cloth, 1s. each.

KEPT FOR THE MASTER'S USE.

THE ROYAL INVITATION; or, Daily Thoughts on Coming to Christ.

MY KING; or, Daily Thoughts for the King's Children.

ROYAL COMMANDMENTS; or, Morning Thoughts for the King's Servants.

ROYAL BOUNTY; or, Evening Thoughts for the King's Guests.

LOYAL RESPONSES; or, Daily Melodies for the King's Minstrels.

STARLIGHT THROUGH THE SHADOWS; and other Gleams from the King's Word.

---

**UNDER HIS SHADOW.** The Last Poems. Super royal 32mo, cloth, gilt edges, 1s. 6d.

**THE MINISTRY OF SONG.** Super royal 32mo, cloth, gilt edges, 1s. 6d.

**UNDER THE SURFACE.** Poems. Crown 8vo, cloth, 5s.; also super royal, 32mo, cloth, gilt edges, 1s. 6d.

## WORKS BY MISS M. V. G. HAVERGAL.

MEMORIALS OF FRANCES RIDLEY HAVERGAL. Recently published. Crown 8vo, with Steel Portrait, and other Illustrations, cloth, 6s.; also a Cheaper Edition, roan, 3s.; cloth, 1s. 6d; paper covers, 6d.

PLEASANT FRUITS; or, Records of the Cottage and the Class. Small crown 8vo, cloth, 2s. 6d.

THE LAST WEEK: Being a Record of the Last Days of Frances Ridley Havergal. 32mo, sewed, 2d.; cloth, 6d.

## ILLUSTRATED BOOKS FOR BOYS.
### BY R. M. BALLANTYNE.
Crown 8vo, cloth, price, 5s.

THE YOUNG TRAWLER, a Tale of Life, Death, and Rescue in the North Sea. Crown 8vo, with illustrations, cloth, 5s.

DUSTY DIAMONDS, CUT AND POLISHED: A Tale of City Arab Life.

THE BATTERY AND THE BOILER; or, The Electrical Adventures of a Telegraph Cable Layer.

THE GIANT OF THE NORTH; or, Pokings round the Pole.

THE LONELY ISLAND; or, The Refuge of the Mutineers.

POST HASTE: A Tale of Her Majesty's Mails.

IN THE TRACK OF THE TROOPS; A Tale of Modern War.

THE SETTLER AND THE SAVAGE; A Tale of Peace and War in South Africa.

UNDER THE WAVES; or, Diving in Deep Waters. A Tale.

RIVERS OF ICE: A Tale Illustrative of Alpine Adventure and Glacier Action.

THE PIRATE CITY; An Algerine Tale.

BLACK IVORY; A Tale of Adventures among the Slavers of East Africa.

THE NORSEMEN IN THE WEST; or, America before Columbus.

THE IRON HORSE; or, Life on the Line. A Railway Tale.

THE FLOATING LIGHT OF THE GOODWIN SANDS.

ERLING THE BOLD: A Tale of the Norse Sea Kings.

THE GOLDEN DREAM: A Tale of the Diggings.

DEEP DOWN: A Tale of the Cornish Mines.

FIGHTING THE FLAMES: A Tale of the London Fire Brigade.

SHIFTING WINDS: A Tough Yarn.

THE LIGHTHOUSE; or, The Story of a Great Fight Between Man and the Sea.

THE LIFEBOAT: A Tale of our Coast Heroes.

GASCOYNE, THE SANDALWOOD TRADER: A Tale of the Pacific.

## ILLUSTRATED BOOKS FOR BOYS. BY R. M. BALLANTYNE.

Crown 8vo, cloth, illustrated, price 3s. 6d.

TALES OF ADVENTURE ON THE SEA.

TALES OF ADVENTURE BY FLOOD, FIELD, AND MOUN-
TAIN.

TALES OF ADVENTURE; or, Wild Work in Strange Places.

TALES OF ADVENTURE ON THE COAST.

TWICE BOUGHT: A Tale of the Oregon Gold Fields.

MY DOGGIE AND I.

THE RED MAN'S REVENGE.

PHILOSOPHER JACK: A Tale of the Southern Seas.

SIX MONTHS AT THE CAPE: Letters to Periwinkle from South
Africa. A Record of Personal Experience and Adventure. With twelve Illustrations
by the Author. A New Edition.

THE MADMAN AND THE PIRATE.

------

THE KITTEN PILGRIMS; or, Great Battles and Grand Victories.
Quarto, paper boards, with numerous illustrations, 5s.

BATTLES WITH SEA. 16mo, cloth, illustrated, 2s. 6d.

THOROGOOD FAMILY. (New Vol. of Miscellany.) 16mo, cloth,
illustrated, 1s.

------

## HOME AND SCHOOL SERIES OF JUVENILE BOOKS.

With Illustrations. In Small crown, extra cloth, each 1s. 6d.

AMOS FAYLE; or, Through the Wilderness into a Wealthy Place.
By Mrs. PROSSER.

RUNNING AWAY.

STORIES OF THE LAND WE LIVE IN. By WILLIAM LOCKE.

A RAY OF LIGHT TO BRIGHTEN COTTAGE HOMES. By the
Author of "A Trap to Catch a Sunbeam."

THE STORY OF AN OLD POCKET BIBLE, as related by itself.
By ROBERT COX, A.M.

ASHTON COTTAGE; or, The True Faith.

MARJORY. By Mrs. MARSHALL.

COURAGE AND COWARDS; or, Who was the Bravest? By the
Author of "The Maiden of the Iceberg."

AGATHA LEE'S INHERITANCE. By Mrs. M. R. HIGHAM, Author
of "The Other House."

NIDWORTH AND HIS THREE MAGIC WANDS. By Mrs. E.
PRENTISS.

HOME AND SCHOOL SERIES OF JUVENILE BOOKS—CONTINUED.

With Illustrations. In small crown, extra cloth, each 1s. 6d.

ALICE L'ESTRANGE'S MOTTO, AND HOW IT GAINED ,THE VICTORY. By RABY HUME.

FAITHFUL UNTO DEATH; or, Susine and Claude of the Val Pelice.

THE BIRTH OF A CENTURY; or, Eighty Years Ago. By Mrs. MARSHALL.

ROSE HARTLEY AND HER CHRISTMAS WAYMAKS. A Tale for Girls leaving School. By Miss C. N. REDFORD.

HELEN HERVEY'S CHANGE; or, Out of Darkness into Light, By MARIA ENGLISH.

SUMMERLAND GRANGE. By LADY DUNBOYNE.

## THE CROWN SERIES.

Crown 8vo, price One Shilling, cloth, Illustrated.

THE BLACK SHEEP OF THE PARISH. By Lady DUNBOYNE.

MRS. ARNOLD. By Miss WODEHOUSE.

THE STORY OF THE REFORMATION, FOR CHILDREN. By Mrs. BOWER.

SCIENCE EVENINGS FOR MY CHILDREN. By the same.

Fcap 8vo, each 1s., cloth. Illustrated.

# NISBET'S ENTERTAINING LIBRARY
### FOR
## YOUNG PEOPLE.

GENTLEMAN JIM. By Mrs. PRENTISS.

FRAMILODE HALL. By Mrs. MARSHALL.

A CHIP OF THE OLD BLOCK. By the same.

THE PRINCE'S BOX; or, The Magic Mirror. By CHRISTINA N. SIMPSON.

URSULA: A Story of the Bohemian Reformation. By M. L. BEKENN.

OUR LADDIE. By Miss L. J TOMLINSON.

VIOLET IN THE SHADE. By Mrs. MARSHALL.

LIGHT ON THE LILY. By the same.

A ROSE WITHOUT THORNS. By the same.

DOLLY'S CHARGE. By Miss BEATRICE MARSHALL.

THE MOUNTAIN MILL. By H. C. COAPE.

FAN'S BROTHER. By Miss BEATRICE MARSHALL.

THE MAITLANDS' MONEY-BOX. By Lady DUNBOYNE.

## CABINET SERIES.
Small crown 8vo, Illustrated.
### Price 2s. 6d.

1. MATTHEW FROST, CARRIER; or, Little Snowdrop's Mission. By EMMA MARSHALL.
2. THE SPANISH BARBER. A Tale. By the Author of "Mary Powell."
3. THREE PATHS IN LIFE. A Tale for Girls. By ELLEN BARLEE.
4. A YEAR WITH THE EVERARDS. By the Hon. Mrs. CLIFFORD-BUTLER.
5. STELLAFONT ABBEY; or, Nothing New. By EMMA MARSHALL.
6. RONALD DUNBEATH; or, The Treasure in the Cave.
7. A SUNBEAM'S INFLUENCE; or, Eight Years After. By the Hon. Mrs. CLIFFORD-BUTLER.
8. A TALE OF TWO OLD SONGS. By the same.
9. ESTHER'S JOURNAL: or, A Tale of Swiss Pension Life. By a RESIDENT. With a Preface by Miss WHATELEY.
10. EFFIE'S FRIENDS; or, Chronicles of the Woods and Shores. By the Author of "The Story of Wandering Willie."
11. THERESA'S JOURNAL. From the French of Madame de PRESSENSÉ. By CRICHTON CAMPBELL.

---

## THE GOLDEN LADDER SERIES.
A Series of Entertaining Books for the Young, principally by the Author of "The Wide Wide World," &c. Crown 8vo, cloth, illustrated, price 3s. 6d.

## THE EIGHTEENPENNY SERIES OF JUVENILE BOOKS,
Suitable for Prizes and Gift Books for Young People. 16mo, cloth, illustrated.

---

## THE SHILLING SERIES OF JUVENILE BOOKS.
16mo, cloth, illustrated.

---

## BALLANTYNE'S BOYS' LIBRARY OR MISCELLANY.
A Series of Seventeen Books. Illustrated. 16mo, cloth, 1s. each; or the set in a neat cloth box, price 18s. 6d.

*A Catalogue of J. N. and Co.'s books, giving a full list of the above series, may be had gratis on application.*

---

LONDON: J. NISBET AND CO., 21, BERNERS STREET.

CPSIA information can be obtained at www.ICGtesting.com
Printed in the USA
LVOW10s1415050514

384487LV00010B/271/P